ANGER MANAGEMENT WORKBOOK

A Step by Step Guide to Take Control of Your Anger and Master Your Negative Emotions

ANTONIO MATTEO BRUSCELLA

COGNITIVE BEHAVIORAL THERAPY SERIES

© Copyright 2020 by Antonio Matteo Bruscella. All rights reserved. The reproduction, transmission, and duplication of any of the content found herein, including any specific or extended information will be done as an illegal act regardless of the end form the information ultimately takes. This includes copied versions of the work, both physical, digital, and audio unless the express consent of the Publisher is provided beforehand. Any additional rights reserved

CONTENTS

PREFACE	1
INTRODUCTION	9
Are you ready for change?	11
CHAPTER I: WHY CBT	17
CHAPTER II: WHAT IS ANGER	25
Myths and Truths of Anger	28
Do You Have an Anger Problem?	32
Types of Anger	36
CHAPTER III: COGNITIVE STRATEGIES	40
Negative Thoughts and Worry	40
Irrational Core Beliefs	42
Faulty Thinking	44
Problem-Solving	50
Cognitive Restructuring	56

CHAPTER IV: BEHAVIORAL STRATEGIES — 61
Anger Log — 61
Imaginal Anger Exposure — 64
In Vivo Anger Exposure — 66
Assertion Training — 72
Time-Out — 78

CHAPTER V: EMOTIONAL AND PHYSIOLOGICAL TECHNIQUES — 80
Mindfulness — 81
Mindful Exercise — 83
Meditation — 85
Deep Breathing — 87
Relaxation — 89

CHAPTER VI: WHAT AN ANGER-FREE LIFE REQUIRES — 91
Time Management — 91
Goal Setting — 94
Diet — 95
Self-Management Strategies — 96
Relapse Prevention — 98

WORKBOOK PAGES — 99
Anger Log — 100
Cognitive Restructuring Worksheet — 101
Contingency Plan Worksheet — 102
Core Belief Worksheet — 103
Identifying and Correcting Distortion — 107
Imaginal Anger Exposure Worksheet — 117
The Relaxation Procedure — 118
Relaxation record — 123
Problem-Solving Worksheet — 124
Relapse Prevention Worksheet — 126

CONCLUSION	128
APPENDIX	130
The Origin and Evolution of CBT	130
The Contemporary CBT Approach	141
The Future Direction of CBT	142
BIBLIOGRAPHY	145
ABOUT THE AUTHOR	151

PREFACE

~

I will be honest: if you have an emotional problem, it can be very difficult to find good help. You may feel trapped, stuck in a rut, continually in conflict with yourself. You may have tried to solve your problems on your own, continually experiencing a sense of failure for not being able to deal with these difficulties; and you may be feeling that after trying everything, there is nothing you can do about it.

If you are like most people, you most certainly know the feeling I am talking about. Sometimes it takes the form of intense despair and a marked sense of helplessness; other times it can take the form of a tormenting doubt—a half-consciousness that you are fighting a losing battle in which defeat is inevitable.

You may have considered talking to someone about it, to vent in order to get a sense of release and feel better because, after all, we have been taught that we need to unblock, let it out, release, or have an in-depth understanding of our discomfort in order to make the negative emotions we feel magically disappear. If you hold such knowledge or beliefs and you want to resolve your emotional difficulties, I can tell you with certainty that you are on the wrong track. For more than twenty years I have been helping people to define and achieve their goals using psychoeducation, psychology, and cognitive-behavioral psychotherapy tools. During these years I have worked in very difficult situations: in prisons, with severe psychiatric pathologies, with the most serious disabilities, and with childhood, adolescent and adult problems.

I have instructed hundreds of psychologists at psychotherapy specialization schools in Italy and trained hundreds of social workers. I currently carry out intense clinical activity in the field of anxiety disorders focusing on strategies that allow people to achieve stable improvements in their lives. I have asked myself if I am doing enough for the patients who ask me for help, how I can best transfer the contents of the psychotherapy sessions, how to best structure the material I give my patients, and how to help people learn in a functional way. I have asked myself many times which strategies are the most effective to produce lasting change in people's lives.

If your daily functioning in your personal, family, social, or work spheres is compromised, I recommend you seek professional psychological support in order to overcome the emotional difficulties afflicting you. However, even if your situation is not dire, you can still benefit from strategies that you can learn and apply yourself in order to obtain improvements in your everyday life or that will allow you to strengthen the work you pursue with a therapist.

The primary strategy is to find self-help material developed by experts who use evidence-based methodologies (Evidence Based Psychology), mainly derived from cognitive behavioral therapy (CBT). This is related to the fact that, among the currently available therapies, CBT is considered one of the most effective therapeutic approaches.

The second strategy is related to the understanding of how learning processes work and, in general, to the factors producing change in people's lives. Indeed, change, from my point of view, comes from necessity through the development of new pathways, namely learning. To deepen this concept, I generally introduce my courses and lessons by asking participants a simple question: "Do you think change is possible?" At first glance, this question surprises everyone because of the triviality of the request, especially if the audience is made up of psychologists, teachers, or social or health workers, and if the training aims to train participants on techniques and strategies in the treatment of disabilities, behavioral disorders, neurodevelopmental problems, or in the intervention of adult psychological disorders. Invariably, I collect a positive opinion from everyone. Next, I invite the participants to reflect on the most common problems concerning their daily lives, their families, and personal and work relationships, and then I pose the same question: how much do you believe that change is possible in relation to these problems? It usually turns out that there is a general perception that issues concerning one's personal life cannot be solved.

This is in stark contrast to the certainty with which many of the participants claim to be able to intervene to bring change to much more serious conditions related to the problems discussed in the courses. I perform this little experiment to underline an aspect that I consider crucial in the work I do, which is the deep conviction that it is always possible to activate paths of change, regardless of the seriousness of the problem one is facing at that moment. I generally tend to ask this question to my patients as well, being aware that one of the most common and annoying features of dealing with the suffering or discomfort caused by a problem is the insidious belief that, basically, "there is nothing I can do about it".

It is important to note that this experience of powerlessness is often triggered in situations where we are considering concrete actions that will require sustained effort, or worse, when we are taking concrete actions to effect change. It is much easier to have self-confidence when our life is going well than when there is a storm. It is difficult to carry out such an important task if we let ourselves be conditioned by misconceptions and disempowering ideas. How many times have you caught yourself questioning beliefs about your abilities? How many times have you said to yourself, "This will never work," or, "Who are you kidding? You know very well that you can't do it." In many cases, self-sabotage can be something habitual which escapes our awareness. Over the years I have developed the view that many people, throughout their struggles to change, subconsciously steer themselves towards defeat.

To explain what I mean by change, I often refer to the following anecdote:

It is 10 o'clock in the morning. Luigi, 6 years old, has decided to learn to ride his new bike without training wheels. Red faced and tense, he gets on the seat, pedals twice, and falls on the cement. Strangely, he does not cry. He recharges himself, gets back on and manages to pedal twice before falling again, this time skinning a knee. But his face relaxes, then he tries again. When his mother calls him for lunch, Luigi has repeated his operation hundreds of times. He has not covered more than 2 meters, but he does not seem disheartened. Rather annoyed by his mother who calls him insistently, he enters the house with bleeding knees, the ideal time to get his wounds medicated. After lunch, he rushes back outside to jump back on the bicycle. He continues the whole afternoon, each attempt followed by some change in posture, some small, imperceptible discovery on how to position his hands and how to balance and coordinate. The darkness is about to arrive when, suddenly, Luigi manages to ride along the whole length of the sidewalk, then... Darn it, he loses control—looking at his feet, he cannot manage to steer and falls. When he gets up again his look is bright, his mood disturbed only by the voice of his mother who calls him back home. The next morning Luigi jumps out of bed. No breakfast for him! Two minutes later he is already on his bicycle. He rides along the length of the sidewalk, then, forgetting to steer, he falls. He stops for a moment and is caught by an intuition: it is a matter of where he is looking. He does not have to look at the pedals or at his feet! So he starts off again, eyes on the road. With the end of the sidewalk approaching, his heart is beating fast. Here it is! He turns the handlebars, looking ahead to where he wants to go, and completes the turnaround. A strong sense of excitement assails him. He is so happy that he gets distracted and falls, but he does not have the time to suffer for the umpteenth skinning nor to get demoralized, as the sense of satisfaction is too great. Before lunch, Luigi covers the whole length of the sidewalk, there and back, on his bicycle. Every now and then he falls, but the falls are becoming more and more predictable, so he learns to prevent the damages by straightening himself during the fall—no more scrapes! His satisfaction is at its peak, and he continues to repeat that path hundreds of times until the evening. The miracle of change has taken place: now he has learned, the learning process is complete. His life has changed, even though this learning may seem trivial.

Observing children develop new skills with impressive rapidity has led me to reflect on the differences in many adults who have great difficulty in approaching change. Putting aside aspects such as neural plasticity and psychophysiology, it is striking to observe how adults seem to have completely lost the ability to approach learning new things in the same spirit.

Making a decision, initiating a process of change, implementing the necessary actions, or moving forward with determination and confidence despite adversity seem to be compromised processes in adults. But how do we become so confused about our ability to learn and change? As adults, every situation that poses a challenge leads most of us to develop concerns about our abilities. We practice self-criticism to the point of convincing ourselves about the truth of our negative evaluations. Contemporary society pushes us towards the pursuit of perfectionism and makes us extremely sensitive to our mistakes. I am convinced that people are capable of achieving spectacular changes in their lives, especially if they abandon the idea of being conditioned by immutable personality traits.

But how is it possible to develop a strong conviction about the possibility of promoting processes of change in oneself or others? I believe that this can only be done by focusing on a few questions: What is our model of change? What do we actually have to do to change or promote change in ourselves or others? In which elements should we intervene? What are the tools at our disposal to promote change? And finally, how can we check our actions to ensure that a change has really taken place?

Throughout this paper I will discuss my answers to these questions and suggest specific self-improvement strategies you can use if you are experiencing intense negative emotions related to ***anger***. Anger has devastating effects on our society, ranging from violence on the streets to violence against women and children—often carried out within the family. Without reaching these extremes, it can be argued that this intense negative emotion affects each of us at various times in our lives, and that for some people it becomes extremely difficult to manage, to the point of compromising one's personal, social, and work functioning. If you are struggling with anger management, this guide will offer you the opportunity to start a step-by-step journey of self-help and to acquire new skills to handle your dysfunctional anger response, providing you with the basis for improving your life on a personal, family or work level.

It's normal to experience anger, and it doesn't mean that there's something "wrong" with you. However, you may experience excessive anger that can make it difficult to enjoy yourself or control your actions. This can become destructive as it causes your mood to down-spiral, you become increasingly negative, and you can behave in ways that you later regret, which might have negative implications on your personal or work life—sometimes the legal authorities even have to get involved! But, it doesn't have to be this way.

Whether you simply want to lessen your negativity and learn to let go of anger in your day-to-day life or have a serious anger problem and have been advised to seek help, you can get the answers and help you are looking for with cognitive-behavioral therapy. But, why choose CBT? Simply put, it is a series of therapeutic methods a century in the making that are all backed by science and clinical study. This means that you can trust CBT to work as it has a long documented history of being effective. You don't have to trust some dubious anger-management method recommended by your mother's friend's hair stylist's son. Instead, you can listen to what actual mental health experts and researchers have proven time and again through impartial science.

Countless people have used CBT to help manage their anger, and you could be the next person to experience the profound improvement! Other books offer dubious methods without sound science, leaving you wondering if you can trust the method. But, with the anger-management techniques of CBT taught in this book, you don't have to worry. You can have faith that if you put in the effort, you will see the results. No matter your gender, age, or situation—you can use the tools in this book to create a positive transformation. It will require effort and persistence. Yet, with empirically-backed tools and methods of cognitive-behavioral therapy, you can achieve your goals. In this book, you will find:

— An in-depth look at why CBT is the best way to manage your anger.
— A look at anger and how it affects you.
— How to tell if you have an anger problem.
— Step-by-step cognitive techniques to restructure your thoughts and deal with faulty thinking, irrational core belief, and negative thoughts.
— Behavioral techniques for assertion training, in vivo and imaginal anger exposure, and creating your own anger log.
— Emotional and physiological techniques including meditation, mindfulness, deep breathing, and mindful physical exercise.
— How to maintain an anger-free life with step-by-step actionable techniques to manage your life.
— Workbook pages to use time and time again.

Why wait to learn to experience an anger-free life? To improve not only your life but the lives of those around you? You don't have to live every day struggling while hot under the collar and trying to keep your cool. Instead, you can pick up this book and start taking steps today to see improvement in as little as a couple of weeks.

INTRODUCTION

∽

Anger is a natural part of the human experience. This is not a bad thing; it is not a wrong emotion to feel. After all, anger can be used for good or bad. A person may use their anger at injustice to work toward a better society. Another person may use their anger to defend a loved one against unfair treatment. Yet another person may use their anger at their own failings to pursue self-growth. Anger is not the enemy—it is all about how the anger it acted on and utilized.

However, many people struggle with their anger. It can be difficult to know how to act on it, and sometimes we develop unhealthy behaviors. For instance, a person may develop road rage due to unmanaged anger. They may yell at their loved ones during arguments, causing further friction and hurt. A person may get so angry that they see red and are hardly able to process what is being said to them. They may even become violent, hitting walls and other inanimate objects, or worse, other people. As you can see, there are many ways that unmanaged anger may develop. Often times, it starts small. But, as a person continues to develop unhealthy coping mechanisms, it worsens. Life doesn't have to be this way.

You can develop healthy coping mechanisms to prevent outbursts, allowing you to know when to use controlled anger for good while also keeping unproductive anger in check. By learning tools to manage your anger, you can improve not only your life but the lives of everyone around you. Whether you are reading this book for yourself or to help someone else, no matter your gender, your age, or your situation—you can use the tools in this book to create a positive transformation. It will require effort and persistence. Yet, with empirically-backed tools and methods of cognitive-behavioral therapy, you can achieve your goals.

No matter how bad your discomfort feels, or how hopeless it may seem at times, you can make things better. You deserve to live a life free from the constant tendrils of negative emotions. You deserve to live a life you can enjoy without worry or fear. You deserve to live a life where you do more than just survive. You can, and you will attain the life you wish to lead with perseverance and effort. No matter how hard things may get, remember to keep your goals in mind, and never stop striving for them. Happiness and mental wellness are within your reach, even if your discomfort has fooled you into thinking otherwise.

It is important to note, however, that while this workbook is designed to provide you with information on cognitive behavioral therapy and suggest some strategies you can utilize to manage your emotions, it is NOT a substitute for a proper diagnosis, treatment, or the advice of an appropriate health professional.

The book is a fantastic reference but will never be able to provide you the individualized care a licensed health professional could offer. If your symptoms are severe or overwhelming, or if you have never seen a doctor about your mental health symptoms, it is important to seek advice from a qualified health professional. Likewise, this book does not advise you to alter any medication that has been prescribed, and you should always seek medical advice before altering your medication regimen. If you ever feel as if you may hurt yourself or others, please consider this a medical emergency and call your local emergency services hotline or seek treatment in an emergency room. Remember, no matter how severe your symptoms may seem or feel, you can fix things. If not through this book, then through seeking help from a licensed therapist or taking medication.

Are you ready for change?

"At some point in our existence we are prepared to recognize the importance of certain things that most unprepared people ignore or underestimate." (Prochaska et. al, 1994). Before going any further, I would like to discuss with you a very sensitive issue that will inevitably affect the benefits you could gain from the material you are reading. If you refer to a specific problem that you have solved during the course of your life, you will realize that this change did not come about suddenly but rather at the end of a process that may have lasted years.

Before deciding to change, you may have ignored your problem, then considered the possibility of dealing with it, and finally reorganized your psychological, physical, and material resources and took action to deal with it. When you finally succeeded in overcoming your difficulties, you worked hard to maintain the benefits you gained and the different self-image you built. If, in the course of this change, you failed, you probably gave up for a while, then you came back fighting for your goal. Authoritative scholars (Prochaska at al., 1994) have found that these kinds of experiences are recurrent and predictable within a change pathway, and that the achievement of a personal growth goal follows defined stages, each characterized by specific challenges and learnings that the person will have to develop from one stage to the next. Each stage does not inevitably lead to the next, and it is possible to jump backwards at any point along the way. Understanding how these stages work will help you to define which stage you are currently in and what specific challenges you will have to face on your path to change. There are six well-defined stages leading to change (Prochaska et al., 1994): Pre-contemplation, Contemplation, Preparation, Action, Maintenance and Exit.

— *Pre-contemplation:* If you are at this stage, you probably have no intention of changing and you will probably deny the actual existence of the problem. Although family, friends, doctors, or work colleagues have clearly noticed the problem, you do not see it as such. You have no intention of changing, even though this change is often strongly advocated by those around you. You may have felt the need to distance yourself from the problem, avoiding discussions about it in newspaper articles, television reports, and any news. When the problem accidentally becomes a topic of conversation, you may have felt an urgent need to change the subject. If you are at this stage, you probably started reading this book because of external pressures. The bad news is that, when the pressure from others recedes, you will quickly abandon this path. You will probably feel a sense of discouragement in some circumstances because talking or reading about the problem will make you feel hopeless. However, if you are experiencing this negative emotion and you recognize it, you are on track to progress to the next stage. Remember that change is possible, and you can use the need to neutralize this negative emotion as a starting point for progressing to the next stages of change.

— *Contemplation:* If you are at this stage, then you might have realized that you have a problem and you might have started to think seriously about solving it. You may feel the need to gain as much information as possible about your problem because you want to know what is causing it before hypothesizing possible solutions. You might have made plans, though not clearly defined, for concrete action in the coming months. The bad news is that, despite your good intentions, you may be a long way from putting your intentions into action. In the contemplation stage, you know your destination and you know how to get there, but you are not yet ready to go. Many people remain in this stage for years. Fear of failure might have led you to feel that you should achieve full knowledge of the problem before acting. At this stage, if you have started to focus on solutions to the problem rather than causes and on the future rather than the past, you are on track towards the next stage. You may also experience feelings of excitement and anxiety as you anticipate the concrete actions you will take.

— *Preparation:* If you are at this stage, you have planned some actions to be carried out in the next months, and you are arranging the last things before you start to act. You might have verbalized your willingness to change to someone else and feel ready to act. However, you may still have doubts about what you are going to do, and you may feel somewhat ambivalent about the change. You need to convince yourself that change is the best solution. Remember that this is a very important step and that gaining a sense of confidence in the choices you are about to make is a fundamental move that will lead you towards your goal, so take the time you require to feel confident; do not rush things, even if you perceive a strong awareness. People who skip this phase and decide to act immediately put themselves at risk of failure. At this stage you can use time to plan your actions more carefully and make sure you understand the importance and significance of the next steps.

— *Action:* If you are at this stage, you may be trying to change your behavior by taking action and making concrete steps to achieve your goal. Action requires effort and energy, and if you have acted correctly, people around you might have noticed your efforts and encouraged, rewarded, and supported you. Efforts made at this stage receive more support from others than during the previous and subsequent stages. However, this does not mean that the other stages are less important. You will need to remind yourself that having taken one step forward does not mean that the desired change has been achieved and that it will be essential to continue working steadily to consolidate and maintain the results achieved. Although behavioral change is the most visible part of change, it is certainly not the only part. Change means reaching a new awareness, reacting emotionally in a new and more functional way, modifying distorted and dysfunctional thoughts, changing your self-image, and so on. Many of these changes will have occurred in earlier stages while others will occur in later stages. Each change from one stage to the next constitutes considerable progress. If you have avoided the problem for years, then you have realized its existence and thought seriously about changing it. This makes the transition between the stage of pre-contemplation to that of contemplation by no means an insignificant one, certainly not less important than the transition between the preparation and action phases.

— *Maintenance:* Even if you are in this advanced stage, you will still face some challenges. In order to maintain and consolidate the progress you have made, you will need to work hard and take time to plan how to prevent a relapse. Change never ends with the action stage. Without hard work in the maintenance phase, you will almost certainly fall back into the pre-contemplation or contemplation phase. Programs that promise to provide change often miss this piece of information: *change is a long and continuous process.*

— *Exit:* The exit stage is the ultimate goal for all people who want to change. In this phase the well-being you have achieved in your life will be safe from temptation or threat, and you will have developed confidence in your ability to prevent possible relapses due to strong environmental stresses or adverse life events, or to face relapses if they occur.

It should be emphasized that change does not take place according to a simply linear model in which one goes through the various stages (or back to a previous stage in the case of a relapse). The model closest to reality for representing change through stages may be that of a spiral. With each recovery after a possible relapse, the diameter of the spiral becomes smaller and smaller and the transition between the stages becomes faster and faster. In this view, relapses are considered only a functional step towards the more stable and lasting change that lies at the apex of the spiral.

Therefore, even if you have failed to achieve change in the past, do not lose heart. You will get the results you want by struggling every day to move from the pre-contemplation phase to the exit of the program by developing an effective relapse prevention strategy and continuing to apply the most effective change techniques. Even if you do everything right, relapse will be the rule rather than the exception. The emotions caused by relapse are not pleasant. You will feel as if you have failed completely. You may suffer a sense of guilt. You may feel as though all your efforts have been in vain, and a demoralizing mood will take over. You will feel the urge to abandon the change completely, and you might slip back into the pre-contemplation stage. Repeated unsuccessful attempts could make you feel that you are in a vicious cycle that leads nowhere.

Please note, however, that this is not a vicious circular cycle but rather a spiral that will lead you to success. A return to the pre-contemplation phase will only represent a narrower turn of the spiral. At each turn you will have opportunities to learn new information and consolidate your learning. An action followed by relapse is far from being the same as a lack of action. Remember that people who have tried to solve their problem in the past month will have double the chance of achieving the result in the next six months than those who have not taken any action.

Change process stages

Think about your personal experiences and the efforts you are making to overcome your difficulties.
Write down in the table the information that is useful, from your point of view, to frame your current position in the stages described above.

Stage	*Explain why you feel you are at this stage and what you think you need to do to progress to the next stage*
Pre-contemplation	
Contemplation	
Preparation	
Action	
Maintenance	

CHAPTER I: WHY CBT

There are many approaches you could take to try to manage your anger for a healthier and better life. So, why choose cognitive-behavioral therapy, otherwise known as CBT? Simply put, you want something that works. You want to use a method that understands that a person's mind and behavior works together to either continue down the path of self-destruction or grow on a path of self-improvement.

The methods used in what is now known as CBT take root one century ago. While the term cognitive-behavioral therapy wouldn't be coined until several decades later, some of the same methods used in CBT today were in use a hundred years ago. The reason for this is because CBT has long been studied, tested, and empirically-proven to be effective. With short-term therapy, a person can gain long-term, lasting results.

Cognitive-behavioral therapy is unique because it understands that our cognition affects our behavior, but our behavior also impacts our cognition. Simply put, the two are caught in a never-ending cycle. All too often, this cycle causes people to get stuck in unhealthy or unhelpful patterns of thought and behavior. But, if you understand how to better impact the cognitive-behavioral cycle, you can put it to good use for personal growth. CBT makes use of that cycle by teaching you tools you can utilize whether you are working with a therapist or on your own. While it may often feel like we are out of control, especially when anger is on the rise, the truth is you have more power than you think—if only you learn how to use it. Your outside circumstances don't dictate how you react. You don't have to be tossed around on the waves of life, allowing your anger to take control.

Instead, you can choose to take control of your circumstances, behavior, and cognition for a healthier and happier life. Not only can CBT help you with anger, but it can also help with: Anxiety; Depression; Addictions; Eating Disorders; Phobias; Personality Disorders; OCD; General Stress. And, this is only the tip of the iceberg! CBT has been empirically-proven and used for decades to manage and treat these conditions and many more!

Whether you are struggling with anger alone or combined with other mental health struggles, you can gain the understanding and help you need through a personalized CBT approach. In order to be able to help a variety of struggles, CBT does not only recognize that your behavior is based on your cognition while also affecting it; CBT also focuses on your current well-being rather than becoming distracted with your childhood or dreams. This is important since many people are left struggling in the here-and-now, but the psychotherapeutic approach they are used to ignores the present and focuses on the past—leaving them at a standstill.

Cognitive-behavioral therapy doesn't ignore your past but rather chooses to focus on how it is affecting your present. For instance, you won't be sitting on a couch telling a therapist about how you were raised for an hour every week. Instead, whether you are working with a therapist or on your own, you will prioritize your current cognitive well-being. This means some of your cognitive thought patterns may arise from your adulthood or your childhood. But, you ultimately treat both forms of unhelpful thought patterns in the same way: you face them head-on and correct them with a healthier and more balanced thought pattern. These negative, unhealthy, or unbalanced thought patterns are one of the bases of CBT and are commonly known as cognitive distortions or distorted thinking. You can develop these distorted thoughts at any point in your life and for a variety of reasons. But, rather than psychoanalyzing why they developed, CBT instead focuses on replacing them with healthy balanced thoughts so that you can overcome your struggles and reach your goals.

There are many cognitive distortions that may cause anger and, in turn, behavioral struggles. Some examples include:

— "They're an SOB."
— "They're always getting in my way."
— "I can't stand them; I'll show them!"
— "They're out to make me miserable."
— "They just don't try hard enough!"
— "I'm going to make them feel guilty for the way they treated me; it serves them right!"
— "They never consider how I feel!"
— "Their procrastination is unacceptable."

Do any of these thought processes sound familiar? While these thoughts are perfectly normal, they are not helpful or balanced. Because of this, they are known as distorted thinking. This doesn't mean the other person is in the right, they could still be in the wrong, but the way you are approaching the situation most likely needs more balance. There are many methods you can use to promote more balanced thinking, overcome distorted thoughts, and develop healthier behaviors. Rather than being a single method, CBT is a collection of methods and techniques that can be customized to an individual person's needs—allowing it to be an effective therapy for a wide range of people and struggles. But, one of the many tools that can be used is Cognitive Reframing. With this method, a person uses a workbook or journal page to examine their thoughts, the consequences of the thoughts, and whether or not they are balanced. This allows a person to truly analyze their thoughts in a way that isn't impeded by emotions such as anger or stress. Once a person has analyzed the thoughts, determining if they are distorted or not, it then helps the person determine the best course of behavior to act on.

Cognitive Reframing can help people with a wide range of struggles, including anger. This method allows a person to calm down, think rationally and with balance, and then act on reason rather than a surge of anger. In later chapters, we will examine distorted thinking and Cognitive Reframing in more depth. You will be able to learn why these thoughts are unbalanced, how to practice Cognitive Reframing, and more. While distorted thinking can accompany anger, that is not to say all anger is caused by distorted thinking. There is just and righteous anger. There are many things in our personal lives or that we might see in the news that can justly make us angry—such as people who are being needlessly cruel. You can experience people in your own life who are outright bullies. It can make you angry for the way they treat us or others. Similarly, you may see about needless death and destruction in the world, as it often seems impossible to escape the ever-constant stream of world-wide news.

The purpose of Cognitive Reframing and other CBT tools is not to gaslight you into doubting yourself or your anger. Instead, its purpose is to allow you to see when your anger is healthy and balanced, and when it is destructive. By gaining this insight into your cognition and anger, you can learn how to better act on your emotions. It will give you confidence in your ability to act with balance. You can learn when to seek justice, forgive, and give grace. You can also learn how to identify if your anger is mistaken so that you don't take it out on someone undeserving. You can learn how to better express and manage your anger, even when it is justified. Just because anger might be deserved or justified doesn't mean we can act on it recklessly. For instance, in an extreme case, anger might be justified at someone who has committed a grievous crime. But, that doesn't mean we can take the law into our own hands to punish the person. Instead, we should follow the law and seek justice through a court of law. While this case may be extreme, there are many everyday situations when anger may be justified but still require temperance.

For instance, if someone cuts you off in traffic, yelling slurs at them and tailgating is not the answer, even if what they did was wrong. You may not be able to control what other people do, but you can control how you react. There are better ways you can handle the situation, and CBT will give you the tools you need to do just that.

One of the core principles of cognitive-behavioral therapy is that it is empirically-backed. Back when it was created during the 1900s, psychotherapists saw the need and importance for a form of therapy that could be scientifically-proven to be effective. At the time, there were many new therapeutic methods popping up, but not all of them could be scientifically proven. A therapist might make claims that the methods were effective with their individual clients, but without scientific-backing, the claims could not be trusted to help people at large.

To create effective and empirically-backed therapeutic methods, the founding creators of CBT looked at official scientific studies to learn about human behavior and cognition. They took these principles and created treatment methods, which were then again scientifically-tested and proven to be effective. These methods continue to be used around the world today to help people with a variety of struggles gain the tools they need to reach their goals. We now have more scientific studies proving the benefits of CBT than ever before. These studies have found it to be an effective method of therapeutic treatment for a wide range of struggles. But, today, we will be looking specifically at how CBT has been scientifically-proven to help people struggling with anger. In a 1999 study on utilizing CBT to treat adult patients with anger issues, it was found to be an effective method. Due to the ability to customize CBT to the individual, the therapists were able to finely tune the tools and methods used to be effective for individual patients. By understanding each patient's unique situation, characteristics, and desire for change, the therapists were able to help the patients learn how to manage their anger and reach their therapeutic goals. In another study, it was found that many patients were not ready for change regarding their anger. This is to be expected because while there are many people who seek positive change when it comes to their anger, that is not always the case.

There are many times a person only seeks therapeutic treatment due to the people in their lives requiring the person to seek therapy—such as a spouse demanding that their partner seek therapy or breakup or even court-mandated therapy. Even in these situations, when a patient is reluctant to change, CBT can be effective. But, before jumping straight into the methods and tools, the therapist must first help the patient become ready for change. Once the therapist is able to help the patient become ready and accepting for change and growth—using CBT methods to help them see how and why growth is a good thing—then they can move onto treating the anger itself. This study found that when therapists understand the need to help their patients become ready and open to therapeutic change, then there can be great benefit and growth.

That CBT is effective, as it allows the therapist to understand each patient's individual needs. Many people experience anger as a result of post-traumatic stress disorder (PTSD). This condition occurs after a person experiences a traumatic event. While it is a common condition, the symptoms can vary widely from person to person, as there are many potential symptoms. In one study, researchers analyzed how effective CBT is for patients with PTSD who struggled with anger. This study analyzed sixty-seven different women who were struggling with PTSD and the resulting anger due to assault. The results were amazing! Not only did CBT help greatly reduce the anger and other PTSD symptoms the women experienced, but it also provided them with helpful coping mechanisms, and they still experienced the benefits at long-term post-treatment checkups. This means that even though CBT is a short-term therapy solution, a long time after their therapeutic sessions had ended, the patients were still seeing a great reduction in their anger and PTSD.

Ultimately, the study was seen as a great success. In yet another study, patients with anger and substance abuse tried cognitive-behavioral therapy. As usual, this study was deemed a success, as the patients experienced a reduction in anger and improved coping skills. This is great news because by improving their anger and other struggles, the person can also lessen their dependency on substance abuse. Lastly, a meta-analysis examining studies of CBT in the treatment of anger in children and adolescents found CBT to be highly effective.

The patients were able to experience improvement in anger, aggressive behavior, problem-solving, social skills, and more. By completing the short-term cognitive-behavioral therapy with a therapist, the patients were able to learn skills that would help them continue reducing their anger and improving how they act on anger long-term. This is great news because it shows that CBT is effective for all ages! If we can help children and adolescents learn how to handle their anger at a young age, then it will set them up for success as they reach adulthood. By helping children learn how to manage their anger, they will experience better relationships, be more successful at work, and be less likely to fall into criminal behavior.

These studies prove that no matter your age, gender, diagnoses, or past—you can benefit from CBT. You can choose to make a better life for yourself and those around you. By being open to change and improvement, you can experience growth like never before. It will take hard work and consistent effort, but countless people have achieved it before, and you can, too. If you want to learn more about the history, theory, and science of CBT, you can read the information enclosed in the appendix of this book.

CHAPTER II: WHAT IS ANGER

If you were to look at the dictionary definition of anger, Merriam-Webster would say that it is: "A strong feeling of displeasure and usually of antagonism.". This definition might give you an idea of what anger is, and a writer might use it when creating a novel, but the true experience of anger is much deeper than any concise definition can simply explain.

If you have been on the receiving end of a person's anger, you understand just how scary it can truly be. A person can begin to yell, be unwilling to listen, and may become overbearing and invade your personal space. Some people even become physically violent—and even if a person doesn't, they may be so close to acting on the violence that those around them are always worried about their safety. Suffice to say, if a person has anger issues, it affects everyone who interacts with them.

People become concerned about their safety, resentful of the way they are treated, and they may even leave the relationship. It isn't uncommon for a person with anger issues to lose friends and family as a consequence of their actions. For the people frequently feeling angry, there are many symptoms of what you could be experiencing. It is not only anger, aggression, and antagonism. You might also feel stressed, irritated, resentful, depressed, or guilty. Likely, your fight-or-flight response is activated and pushing you to either want to escape the situation or fight back verbally or even physically. Anger is not only an emotional and cognitive response; it has physical side-effects, as well. For example, you may begin to feel dizzy, light-headed, or hot. You may begin to shake, clench your jaw, grind your teeth, sweat excessively. You might even develop a headache or stomachache.

People often begin to yell, cry, become sarcastic, rub their heads, fist their hands, and you might even develop a craving for a relaxing substance such as alcohol or a cigarette. Perhaps you are reading this book for yourself; if so, consider writing down a list of how anger affects you personally. Consider the list above and which of these side-effects you experience. How do you feel emotionally? What physical symptoms do you experience? How do you take your anger out on those around you?

If you are reading this book in hopes of helping someone else with their anger issues, consider writing out a list of how their anger issues affect you. What do they say or do when angry that burdens you? Do they yell? Become sarcastic? Behave in a way that threatens violence? Write down both what they do and how those actions make you feel. You might feel scared and sad. You may feel the need to escape them.

If the person is open to improvement and willing to listen to your troubles, then showing them a list of how their actions affect you may help. Of course, this varies based on the individual people and situations involved, so only you can decide if this is the best course of action. While anger can be scary—whether you are the person experiencing the emotions of anger or you are being affected by another person's anger—it is a natural and important human emotion. But, it is important to understand that when you are emotionally angry, that is not the only thing you are feeling. Depending on why you are feeling the emotion of anger, you can also be experiencing various cognitive feelings. These are different than emotions, as they are your cognitive thoughts. For instance, while you may be feeling the emotion of anger, your cognitive feelings/thoughts might be those of fear, anxiety, disappointment, embarrassment, envy, or many others.

Understanding the cognitive feelings behind your anger is important because only by understanding these feelings can you address the cause of your anger head-on. By addressing these feelings, you can, in turn, better address the emotions. You might be reading this book to help with your own anger issues, or not. There are many children and adolescents who struggle with anger, and it is the duty of the adults in their lives to help them through it. If you are helping such a child, it is important to remember the distinction between their emotion of anger and the cognitive feelings behind the anger.

When you are dealing with someone who is angry and possibly volatile, it can be difficult to remain calm, analyze the situation, and help them through it. After all, your own fight-or-flight system is trying to cause you to take action to protect yourself. In this case, you can use CBT tools not only to help the child but to help yourself remain calm, as well. Try to remember that the child is angry because of unresolved feelings. These feelings may be justified, or they could be caused due to distorted thinking. Either way, the child needs help processing their feelings and reframing their cognition so that they can let go of their anger and learn coping tools.

Remember, anger is a natural human emotion that expresses an unmet cognitive, emotional, or physical need. By addressing the cause of a child's anger and teaching them CBT coping mechanisms, you can help the child overcome their anger. Although this is not only true for children and adolescents, it is true for adults, as well.

Myths and Truths of Anger

When it comes to anger, there are many common misunderstandings and myths. These are important to learn about because you need to understand the truth of anger, whether you are hoping to overcome your own anger or hope to help someone else with theirs. We will be dealing with each myth and the truth behind it in turn, so get ready to learn!

Anger is Bad

While it may be easier to simply classify anger as "bad," especially if you have been on the receiving end of a person's anger, this is not necessarily true. Anger is an emotion, just like happiness and sadness, and this means that anger itself isn't something to be scared of or ashamed of. What matters is how a person uses their anger. After all, happiness and sadness can be used poorly, as well. This may be more difficult to imagine, but there are many cases in which a person may utilize other emotions poorly.

For example, a person may become happy by bullying others, but this obviously is the morally wrong choice. A person who is sad may take out their feelings on those around them, throwing out unkind words like daggers and then justifying the harm done because they are sad. Just as people can act poorly based on other emotions, a person can choose to use anger for good, as well. A person might use their anger at the injustice of homelessness to start up a local community home for those in need. They may use their anger at people who abuse animals to propel them to rescue animals in need. Or, they might use their anger at someone who is being cruel to a friend to stand up for their friend, supporting them and having their back. Just like any other emotion, anger serves a purpose. The emotion itself is not morally equivalent; what matters is how you act on it.

Anger is Good

Many people develop a toxic idea of strength and independence that relies on utilizing anger to hurt those around them. These people often see anger as a good thing, but they weaponize it so that it becomes harmful. Often, when anger is used in this toxic way, it will lead to property damage, domestic violence, sexual abuse, and more. Just as anger is not necessarily bad, it is not necessarily good, either. But, these toxic behaviors people act on are definitely not good. But, the good news is that this book will teach you better ways to deal with your anger.

Anger isn't a Problem if it's Suppressed

You have most likely known someone in your life who outwardly expressed their anger loudly—likely with unhealthy and toxic behaviors. Most often, when a person thinks of anger management, they think of those types of people.

However, not everyone expresses their anger loudly; some people try to keep it bottled up quietly. In fact, an estimated ninety percent of people bottle up their anger. When doing this, they might deny the anger to others, saying "I'm really not angry," when the truth is that that they are; they might be in self-denial about their anger; or, perhaps they simply refuse to discuss the matter.

While these people may be quieter about their anger, the truth is that their anger matters just as much. They need anger management just as much as anyone else. The reason for this is because even if they are suppressing their anger, it will still interfere with their relationships, how they view the world, and it can even negatively affect your health. Nobody should have to go through life always angry, and CBT can help with that.

Men are Angrier than Women

Studies show that while people frequently think of men as angrier than women, this simply is not true. However, they can experience anger differently. In studies, women tend to get angry just as often as men—about twice a week for those without anger issues. Although, the way they experience this anger can be different. In many cases, while men experience more short-term intense anger, women tend to experience longer anger at slightly less intensity.

Think of the anger difference as a flame. This flame has a fuel source, and this source allows for a specific amount of flame before it is used up. If you speed up the rate of burning, you will get a more hot and intense flame, but the fuel will be used up more quickly. On the other hand, you can slow down the burning so that the heat of the flame is less intense, but it lasts longer.

Neither one of these choices changes how much fuel (or anger) there is, but the way it is experienced is different. This is much like the difference between anger in men and women. Although, remember that this may not always be the case, there are always individual differences and variances. This is only a generalization and may not apply to all people.

Only _____ People Deal with Anger

It is easy to think that only certain types of people deal with anger—especially if you have not been around those types of people when they had reason to be angry. But, the truth is that everyone deals with anger. It doesn't matter their gender, race, nationality, age, or job. Anger is something that everyone experiences, and believing otherwise can put an undue burden on a person. If a person feels that they have no right to be angry because of unrelated factors such as race or gender, then it only makes them feel guilty for being human.

Anger is just in the Mind

Many people believe anger is all in the mind. But, if you experience regular anger, you likely know that this is not true—it has a physical aspect. When a person is angry, it can feel like there is something squeezing their chest or like there is something inside them trying to burst out. Their muscles clench, their jaw becomes tight, their body heat increases, the hairs on their neck and arms stand up, their heart rate and breathing speed up, blood pressure increases, even your blood sugar levels are affected! It is no wonder people struggle to know what to do with their anger when it is affecting them not only emotionally but physically as well.

Anger is About Conflict or Revenge

It's easy to think that anger is based on conflict or revenge, as many people associate anger with arguments or other forms of conflict, such as road rage. But, while anger can certainly lead to increased conflict, there are many times when a person experiences anger without another individual being involved. Even if a person is alone at home, with no other people to conflict with, they can still experience anger. A person's anger may be influenced by bodily pains, loud noises, offensive noises, or even the temperature.

None of these situations are about conflict or revenge, yet a person can still become angry based on the circumstances. The reason for this is because anger is not caused by outward circumstances, such as a person's environment or other people, but by their cognition. What a person believes and their thought patterns that they hold in their cognition influence whether or not they become angry.

This is why one person may become angry when they stub their toe, and another person won't. It is not our circumstances that cause anger, rather our cognition. This is good news because you have the power to change your cognition, allowing you to lessen your anger even if you can't change your circumstances.

Do You Have an Anger Problem?

It can be hard to know if you have an anger problem. When you live with an experience, it just seems normal because it's what you are familiar with. This is why many people don't seek anger management until the people in their lives bring the subject up. This could mean that you are taking the initiative yourself because you noticed your child, friend, or spouse are apprehensive around you because of your anger. Maybe someone had a talk with you, bringing up that you might have a problem and need help. Or, it could have gotten to the point that your job or even a court require anger management.

Whatever brings you here, you are likely wondering if you have a problem; or, if you already know you have one, how bad is it? In this section, you will discover the answers you are looking for. By understanding where you stand, you can then better address the issues.

Anger is an emotion that everyone experiences. Just as everyone will experience happiness, joy, sadness, fear, disgust, and excitement at some point in their lives, they will also experience anger. Of course, the frequency that people experience these emotions vary from person to person. One person may feel happy most of the time, while another might usually feel sad. In the same way, the frequency and depth of anger people feel will vary.

One person may rarely feel angry, with it being an unusual and notable occurrence. But, if you are reading this book, it is likely that you experience anger more frequently or know someone who does. When determining the frequency and intensity of your anger, it is important to understand a few things. Firstly, anger and hostility are not the same things. They may occur together at times, but this is not always the case. Anger is a transient emotion that you experience. On the other hand, hostility is an attitude of mistrust, cynicism, ill will, and paranoia. Secondly, just because you experience anger doesn't mean you always act on it. You may feel angry every day of the week but only act out on the behavior occasionally.

On the other hand, some people might act out in violence a majority of the time they become angry. When calculating the intensity and frequency of your anger, don't base it on your behavior. This is important because you can be angry without acting out on it, and if you don't count these times in your calculation, then you will not be getting a truthful picture. To start with, you should determine how frequently you get angry. Don't only consider the times when you get intensely angry, such as a hot-headed rage.

Any time you get angry at all, even if only a little, counts. People tend not to count the little times or the times that they kept their anger under control, but these times still apply. They are still a part of your lived experience. Often times, people underestimate how frequently they experience anger. This is especially true for those with poor memory or those who simply don't see their anger as a notable experience to remember. Part of this is because if you remember the reason you are angry, you are likely to become angry again, so you try to put it behind yourself and forget it. But, when this happens, it will interfere with calculating your anger frequency.

To get around this problem, you can take a week or two and every time you experience any anger at all, write it down. You can write it in a notebook or on your phone, but make sure you mark it down. For best results, write down the date, time, and intensity of the anger, as this will give you the most accurate results for your calculations. Lastly, remember to be honest with yourself. It is easy to want to underestimate how frequently we feel angry because most people don't like that side of themselves. They don't want to admit that they are frequently angry and might take it out on those around them. But, you can only grow if you first see yourself as you truly are. Looking at the past month, how frequently have you gotten angry or irritated?

— Not at all.
— Once weekly.
— Twice weekly.
— Three to five times weekly.
— Once daily.
— Twice daily.
— Three to five times daily.
— Six or more times daily.

If you experience a four on the above scale, then your anger is worrisome, and it is a good idea to take steps to improve your management. If your anger is a five or higher, then you definitely have an anger problem. The good news is that no matter where you fall on the scale, the CBT techniques and methods in this book can help you. Now that you have an understanding of how frequently you become angry let's look at the intensity of your anger. Again, you need to evaluate yourself honestly; otherwise, you can't expect to grow and improve. Of course, every time you get angry, it won't be to the same degree.

Sometimes, you might get only moderately angry, and other times it might be a rage. Therefore, when calculating the intensity of your anger, take some time to consider what your usual level would be. While there is likely to be variance in the intensity, you will also likely have one level of anger that you experience more frequently than others. For example, if you were to calculate your anger on a number from one to ten—with one being the least angry, five being moderate, and ten being a hot-headed rage—then you might find that your usual anger level is a six or seven. Ask yourself, between one and ten, what is your usual anger level? Before continuing, take some time to thoughtfully consider your answer. Be honest with yourself. If your anger is usually a five or higher, then you likely have an anger problem. Of course, you can have an anger problem even if your usual level is at a four if you are experiencing that four a majority of the time. You have to understand that the frequency and intensity work together—this means that even if your intensity is low, it can still be a problem if you have a high frequency or vice versa.

While it may be hard to see a one to three as a problem, as it is so much less than a ten, if a person is usually at a three, it can be quite a problem! While this person may not be at full-blown anger, but occasionally, they might always be at a constant irritable three. Because of this, when you try to talk to them, they may be short and snappy with you. They may be unlikely to listen. They might always sigh and act exasperated when someone else is talking. They might blame all their problems on other people. While the three on the scale might not be as intense as the higher numbers, if the person is at this irritable level frequently, it can be just as much as a problem.

To understand how your anger frequency and intensity work together, Dr. W. Doyle Gentry developed a great tool. This tool allows you to easily figure out what type of anger you experience based on the intensity and frequency that you have just figured out. It is really simple to use! With the table below, simply add in the information you just calculated. For instance, if your intensity is seven and your frequency is less than once a day, then that means you usually experience episodic rage. On the other hand, if your intensity is three and you experience it at least once a day, then you experience chronic irritation. Have a look at the table and calculate where you place in it. After you are done, we will have a look at what these types of anger mean for you.

Types of Anger

Intensity	Frequency		
	1-3	4-6	7-10
Less Than Once a Day	Episodic irritation	Episodic anger	Episodic rage
At Least Once a Day	Chronic irritation	Chronic anger	Chronic rage

Which of the categories in the table did you fall into? Remember, this is meant to reveal your typical state of anger; it doesn't mean you will never fall outside of that. For instance, while you might generally have chronic irritation, it doesn't mean you won't ever experience episodic rage. Now that you have your typical state calculated, let's have a look at what each of the options means.

Episodic Irritation

Studies have found that most people experience episodic irritation. These people don't get angry or irritated often, and when they do, it is unlikely to be very intense. They are most likely rather easygoing and cheerful, though, like anyone, they will have their own emotional ups and downs. These people don't have anger issues—so, if you are reading this book, this is likely someone you know, but not you yourself.

Episodic Anger

Those reading this book are likely to fall either into episodic anger or the following categories. If you are categorized as episodic anger, then you likely get angry on occasion, but not as frequently as you could—maybe two or three times a week at most. You might get mad when someone cuts you off in traffic, if you spill your coffee, or feel disrespected. This category is still rather common. Your anger is likely not overly toxic, although you could still benefit from CBT techniques.

Episodic Rage

This category is classified by Dr. W. Doyle Gentry—who created this classification system and the above table—as a toxic form of anger. This form of anger puts everyone around you on edge. They are always waiting for what will inevitably set you off like a ticking time-bomb. Your rage sends you over the edge, and you inevitably end up hurting those around you, either through your words or even physically. Many people with episodic rage would deny having a problem, so you must look at yourself honestly and clearly, accepting your faults to see whether or not this applies to you.

Chronic Irritation

Chronic irritation is much like episodic irritation, but rather than happening only occupationally; it is something a person experiences on a daily basis. It is not toxic like episodic rage, but it can still be difficult. Often times, people with chronic irritation are seen as moody or b**chy. People tend to shy away from those with chronic irritation, not wanting to deal with their usual attitude.

People with chronic irritation can sometimes flock together, as some of them can enjoy having people that they can freely discuss their irritation of others without push-back. In this way, the negative behaviors can feed off of each other and grow worse. Chronic irritation may not be as toxic as other forms of anger, but like all forms of chronic anger, the regularity of it causes problems. Not only can it interfere with your enjoyment of life, but it can also cause distance between you and friends and stunt your professional career. Thankfully, as with all forms of anger, CBT can help.

Chronic Anger

Many people reading this book will likely fall into chronic anger, which is the second form of toxic anger. With this form of anger, a person finds themselves in an angry state (four to six on the scale) on a daily basis. They might get angry while driving, shopping, at work, or just when discussing the day's events with their spouse or friend. A person with chronic anger likely knows that they get angry more than the average person, but they still justify it because they don't usually go into a rage. But, the truth is that this form of anger is still toxic. It will damage your relationships, your professional life, and your own mental well-being. Simply put, it is damaging.

Chronic Rage

The last of the six categories, and the most volatile, is chronic rage. Just like with episodic rage, a person with chronic rage will fly off the handle. A person who goes into a rage may not even remember what they said at the time, but it is sure to have been something damaging that those around them won't forget. A person with chronic rage takes it out on everyone around them, whether verbally or physically; it is harmful either way. This type of anger serves no purpose and only works like a weapon that does harm to anyone who may be in your life. A person with chronic rage desperately needs anger management, both for their own sake and the sake of anyone that knows them. Thankfully, if this is you, then you have already taken the first step by starting this book. To take the next step, continue reading and put the following chapters into practice.

By this point, you should have a better understanding of your anger. But, if you are struggling to see yourself honestly and clearly, then try asking the people in your life. Of course, these people might not always feel safe opening up honestly, in fear that you will react out of anger at the truth. This means you will need to create a safe environment for them to talk. Be vulnerable; let them see that you are trying to grow and improve. Guarantee that no matter what they say, you won't get angry. If you do all this and they still are too scared to open up, then you will have to prove to them through your actions. Begin practicing the CBT techniques regularly, allow them to see your hard work and growth, and maybe then they will finally be able to trust you enough to have an honest conversation. Just remember that you are not owed their honesty regarding how your anger has affected them. They have likely been hurt over the years through your anger, and you can't put another burden on their shoulders to then talk to you about it. You can offer them a sincere apology, but it is not your right to demand forgiveness.

CBT is a short-term therapy solution with long-term benefits, but always keep in mind that the relationships you have harmed over the years with your anger will not heal overnight. But, things can improve and get better if you put in the effort.

CHAPTER III: COGNITIVE STRATEGIES

Anger affects you physically through changes such as heart rate and blood pressure, and it can affect your behavior, such as how you speak to a person and the choices you make. However, at its core, anger issues are a cognition issue. The reason CBT is so effective in anger management is precisely because it understands this distinction. Now, this doesn't mean behavioral therapy practices don't have a place in anger management; after all, CBT is all about combining cognitive and behavioral principles. When using CBT, the goal is to change your behavior by making changes to your cognition, and in turn, change your cognition by making changes to your behavior. This may seem complex, but I promise you, the methods and tools are simple to understand and put into place. Once you put these methods into practice, you will begin to see the change and understand how your cognition and behavior affect one another.

Negative Thoughts and Worry

The amount of worry a person experiences can greatly vary—some people worry little, whereas others are seemingly unable to escape their worries. While many people tend to only think of anger as flying into a rage, the truth is that there are many emotions and thoughts behind anger. For many people with anger issues, worry is one of the contributing cognitive factors to their anger. They worry and fear about what might be, whether with their personal lives and relationships, health, or job.

This worry causes a person to become more irritated, potentially causing an intense rage in time. But, while a person is justified in being worried, I would never diminish their worry or the cause for the worry—the truth is that oftentimes what people worry about never occurs. For instance, you may be worried you will be fired if you are late for work, but nothing happens, and things go on as normal. You may worry about your health, but the tests reveal you are fine. This doesn't mean your previous worry was trivial, but it does go to show that everything you worry about isn't bound to happen.

I find that one of the most effective ways to deal with negative thinking and worry is through journaling. You can keep a notebook easily accessible at all times, and whenever you find yourself worrying, take a few minutes to write about it. After you write about your problems and worries, allowing yourself to express what emotions you are feeling and why you are feeling them, then try to put a positive spin on it. For example, take a look at this journal entry:

Worry

I am worried that I will be late for work and my boss will get mad at me and it will affect my income. What if I get fired? This makes me feel scared and anxious. I'm worried that because of these feelings, I will be short and rude when interacting with people.

Positive

Even if I am late for work, I can work more quickly to catch up. My boss may not be happy, but I can explain the situation to them. They have been reasonable in the past, so I have every reason to believe they will be reasonable today, as well. I have proven to be capable in the past, so even if I run into problems, I know I can handle them. While I may be stressed and worried, I have the CBT tools I need to calm down and talk to people calmly and kindly. I don't have to allow my anger or worry to get the better of me. I am in control of my actions, and I choose to continuously learn and do better.

After creating a journal entry like this, you will likely feel relieved and encouraged. The worry and negative thoughts will slowly melt away, and as you continuously prove your capabilities to yourself and practice CBT, then you will find this even easier to accomplish.

Irrational Core Beliefs

We all hold deeply held beliefs—about the world, others, and ourselves. These are known as core beliefs, and they are what we believe above all else. For instance, one person may believe that people are ultimately good and simply make mistakes, while another person may believe that people are ultimately selfish and only watching out for themselves. These are core beliefs that will affect how a person behaves and thinks. A person who believes everyone is ultimately out to get them is less likely to trust others.

They may struggle with negative thoughts. If a person has unbalanced or negative core beliefs, they are more likely to experience problems. This is because your thoughts can become a self-fulfilling prophecy. You believe people are bad. Therefore you are more likely to develop unhealthy relationships. Of course, this not only applies to people who have negative beliefs regarding the world. If a person believes that everyone in the world is ultimately good and simply makes mistakes, they are more likely to excuse toxic behavior in relationships, potentially ending up in abusive situations.

What does this mean about your core beliefs? Simply put, it is important to have a balance. To understand that there is both good and bad in the world, that we make mistakes, but we can also succeed. By identifying and confronting your core beliefs, you can overcome your irrational thoughts and bring balance to your beliefs. Of course, core beliefs are held so deeply that they are more difficult to change than our fleeting thoughts. This is because they are formed throughout our lives and our lived experiences.

Many of these core beliefs are formed during childhood, though they can continue to develop into adulthood. This is why many people who experience abuse as children continue to fall into abusive situations as adults. Core beliefs are meant to help us make sense of the world and ourselves, but when we develop irrational or faulty core beliefs, they will only cause us pain unless we work to overcome them with balanced and healthy new core beliefs. There are many different types of core beliefs a person may hold, but when it comes to irrational core beliefs about themselves, according to Dr. Judith Beck, there are three categories:

— Unlovable
— Helplessness
— Worthlessness

This means that if you hold an irrational or negative core belief about yourself, it fits into one of these three categories and will negatively affect your thoughts and behavior. The way the thoughts and behavior present themselves differently depending on the person, but for the people reading this book, it likely reveals itself through anger. You may become angry at yourself, others, or even the world at large because of these core beliefs. It is easy to overlook core beliefs, as we are more likely to notice our automatic thoughts that we experience throughout the day on a regular basis. But, these automatic thoughts are based on our core beliefs. Imagine that our core beliefs are the soil and nutrients of a garden and your automatic thoughts are the seeds.

These seeds are buried in the soil, and whether they grow healthy or wither is all based on the quality of the soil's nutrients. A person may focus on the plant, but if they ignore the soil, then it will never grow healthy. In order to discover your core beliefs, you can analyze your recurring automatic thoughts. We can all experience a negative thought from time to time, but if we have a recurring negative thought, then that means it is based on an irrational core belief that we need to address. It is much like how a gardener will analyze a plant to determine what ails it. By watching unhealthy growth patterns, you can see that the plant might not have healthy soil.

The understanding will allow you to improve the health of the soil, which will, in turn, improve the health of the plant. Socratic questioning is a great method to uncover and address your irrational beliefs. This process of questioning allows you to analyze your automatic thoughts, determine if they are balanced or detrimental, and uncover the core beliefs beneath them. By practicing this method regularly when you are struggling with negative thoughts, you can actively focus on improving your core beliefs rather than allowing them to unconsciously impede your mental well-being. Use the Core Belief worksheet at the end of this book whenever you find yourself struggling with repeated negative thoughts. For instance, if you find yourself repeatedly thinking, "I'm a failure," "I can't trust anyone," or any other negative thoughts, then practice the worksheet.

Faulty Thinking

Irrational core beliefs, as we have just discussed, can lead to negative automatic thoughts—otherwise known as faulty thinking. We all have automatic thoughts on a daily basis, some positive, others negative, and even others that are neutral. But, when these faulty thoughts are unbalanced, they are known to be cognitive distortions that are unhelpful. These distortions or faulty thoughts influence how we feel about ourselves, others, and the world, and in turn, influence how we feel and behave.

A single faulty thought can wreak havoc in our lives if we choose to believe it and act on it. For instance, if you believe that everyone is out to get you, then you may lash out in anger at those around you, destroying relationships and potentially affecting both your personal and professional areas of life. In CBT, there are ten cognitive distortions or faulty lines of thinking that have been identified. This means that any faulty idea you may hold onto will fit into one of these ten categories. These categories are helpful to know because if you can see that your faulty idea falls into one of these, you can more easily see that it is, in fact, faulty. It is human nature to hold onto our ideas and what we believe to be true, but if you can accept that your idea is a cognitive distortion from this list, then you can work to overcome it and replace it with a more balanced and helpful thought. The ten cognitive distortions include:

Overgeneralization

It's easy to overgeneralize after we experience a negative event. For instance, if you had a toxic experience at one job, it would be easy to overgeneralize and believe that "all" jobs will be just as toxic. If your significant other cheated on you, it would be understandable to believe that you can't trust people and that anyone would cheat on you. But, while this type of overgeneralization is understandable, it is not balanced, accurate, or helpful. The truth is that bad things happen, but so do good things. By overgeneralizing, you are only allowing yourself to expect or see the negative.

All-or-Nothing Thinking

Many people struggle with black-and-white thinking, which is also known as all-or-nothing thinking. With this cognitive distortion, a person tends to believe things are either all good or all bad. They are a complete success or a complete failure. This type of thinking is harmful because a person misses out on the nuances—for instance, a person who a recovered alcoholic might succumb to temptation and have a drink. With all-or-nothing thinking, they might believe that they are a complete failure for giving in, rather than seeing all their prior success. Yes, they might have given in on one day, but countless other days, they resisted. Rather than going off the deep end and continuing to drink because they "failed," they can choose to see their prior success and once again continue to abstain from drink.

Discounting the Positive

With this mental distortion, a person will ignore or refuse to see the positives in their lives. For instance, if a person applied to five colleges and got into three of them, they may discount all the positives of getting into three of their choices because they didn't get into two of them. It's understandable to be disappointed when something you hoped for didn't happen or something negative occurs in life, but if you allow that to block you from appreciating the positives in life, then it is unbalanced, unhealthy, and a distortion.

Magnification

With the magnification distortion, a person magnifies the negative while minimizing the positive. For instance, a person may magnify the negative aspects of a relationship (such as with their parents) while minimizing the positive. This can lead the person to lash out, ignoring any growth their parents have made and instead magnifying the intensity of any negative actions the parents might make. In one example, if the parent accidentally interrupts the person during conversion and apologizes for the mistake, the person might minimize the apology and attempt to reconcile while over-exaggerating the mistaken interruption.

Mental Filters

Mental filtering is similar to overgeneralization, but also the opposite. For example, when a person overgeneralizes, they focus on one negative event and believe it to be more prominent than it truly is. However, with mental filtering, a person chooses to focus on a single event, disregarding all else. Going back to the addiction example, a person who regularly chooses to drink at social events may focus only on the times they have chosen to drink at such events, filtering out all the good times they didn't drink and still had a good time. Just like an overgeneralization, this creates unbalanced and unhealthy thought processes.

Jumping to Conclusions

Jumping to conclusions comes in two forms. First, a person may jump to conclusions about what another person is thinking. For example, you may believe a person is looking down on you or dislikes you even though you don't have proof that's what they are thinking. Second, a person may jump to conclusions by assuming what the future holds—this is known as fortune-telling. With this, a person assumes what will happen in the future, often assuming the worst. For example, they may assume their significant other will leave them. The person will often try to avoid the negative assumption of the future, but by doing this, their behavior often only sets them up for failure or disappointments. In this case, a person may assume their significant other is going to leave them, so they stop even trying to make the relationship work, or they choose to leave the relationship first. This ensures the relationship doesn't work out, all because the person jumped to conclusions.

Emotional Reasoning

One common form of cognitive distortion, especially for people who feel emotions deeply, is emotional reasoning. With this form, a distortion, a person judges their surroundings, other people, or themselves based entirely on their emotions. For example, a person with depression may hate themselves, and because of this emotion, they may then believe that everyone hates them and that they are worthy of being hated.

This is easy to feel when you are depressed, but that doesn't make it true. Similarly, a person may feel unheard by a person, and that may lead them to think negatively about the other person and as if talking is pointless. Now, it is important to realize that this doesn't mean a person's emotions are unimportant—that's not true in the least! Simply put, you need balance. You can take your emotions into account while still weighing them against logic and reason.

With the above examples, if you hate yourself from depression, then you should use various CBT methods and worksheets to help you work through the emotions. If you feel unheard by a person, then there are methods you can try to both improve communication and work through your emotions regarding the situation rather than giving up entirely and viewing it as pointless. Perhaps by explaining to the person how you feel, they will understand you better, and you can work through your struggles.

Labeling

With the labeling distortion, a person will label themselves or others rather than acknowledging the nuances of the situation. For instance, they may label themselves as a "bad" or someone else as "mean," rather than acknowledging that a person has many qualities and one single quality or mistake doesn't define them. This means someone may make mistakes from time to time—as we all do—but that doesn't mean that they are "bad" or "mean." Instead of labeling, it is important to look at a person as a whole.

Personalization and Blame

With the personalization and blame distortion, you begin to place complete blame for a given situation on either yourself or someone else. This occurs when the blame is placed unfairly, as there are other contributing factors at play that a person is ignoring. For instance, a child may blame themselves for the divorce of their parents when any adult looking at the situation rationally knows that there is no way in which the divorce is the child's fault.

"Should" Statements

Lastly, we have "should" statements. These are often self-defeating statements we make against ourselves. For instance, you might get mad at yourself, saying, "I should have been able to get my entire to-do list done," "I should be able to handle my workload without problems," or "I should have been able to meet my weight loss goal!" These are all statements against ourselves, claiming what we believe we "should" be able to accomplish. But, if we fail to meet up to these goals, we become disheartened. These statements are often unforgiving and don't account for problems outside of our control. For instance, maybe you wanted to lose a certain amount of weight within a week, but you didn't. That's okay! It could be that your metabolism was simply slower that week, that your body was working harder than you could tell, or maybe you had to go off of your diet because of a stressful life event—all of that is okay! You can try again another week. If you didn't meet a work goal, that could be frustrating, but you can forgive yourself for mistakes, accept that there are some things outside of your control, and make a plan to account for problems in the future. Similarly, you may create "should" statements for other people, such as "they should know better," "they shouldn't have done that," or "they should do things my way." Again these statements are unforgiving, unbalanced, and unhelpful. These cognitive distortions are important to understand and keep in mind when you are completing workbook pages from the end of this book. When you are using methods to examine your thoughts, go over this list of ten distortions to ensure you aren't struggling with faulty thinking. It is easy to fall into these thought traps, so you just may find that your thinking isn't balanced. Of course, this does not mean that your feelings and thoughts aren't valid, but it does mean that they can use a little more balance to become helpful and healthy.

Problem-Solving

Many people develop anger as a result of problems in their lives. Whether it is spilling your coffee, being late for work, or relationship problems—the truth is we all have problems in our lives. It can be difficult to know how to manage these problems, so when you are prone to anger, you tend to default to feeling anger and expressing it when you run into these problems. The good news is that by using problem-solving tools, you can resolve the problems and often rid yourself of the anger. As you regularly use problem-solving skills, you will likely find yourself getting angry less often when problems do occur because you cognitively understand that you have the tools you need to correct the problem without anger. Of course, it sounds easy to say you will solve a problem, but how is this actually done? There are many problems that you might not have the slightest clue as to how to fix, which is precisely why it is a problem! Don't worry; there is a six-step process to help.

Step One: Identifying the Problem

When you are faced with a problem, it is important to be able to understand how and why things have gone wrong so that you can then set them right, if possible. Even if you can't fix the situation itself, you can still improve how you handle the situation if you see it clearly. Using either a notebook or the problem-solving workbook page from the end of this book, write down everything you believe to be wrong. While you may want to speed up the process by doing this mentally, it is important that you write it all down. This is because the brain processes information differently when you write as opposed to thinking—this is one reason why it is helpful to take notes when studying.

I urge you to use the workbook page or a notebook, it may take slightly more time, but it will be more effective. When writing down your problem, be sure to write down the entire situation, including what is happening, who is involved, and what is going or went wrong. Once you write down the outward problems and influences, continue to write down how these problems are affecting you internally. This means you need to write down how you feel about the problems and why. For instance, you may write that you are feeling "stressed from the conflict" and "don't know how to fix things," which makes you feel "overwhelmed."

Step Two: Identifying Your Goals

Once you understand your problems, then you need to set a goal. For instance, if your problem is that you are in an argument with another person, then your goal might be to come to an understanding, resolve the conflict, and resolve any hurt feelings that arose on either side. You want your goal to be as specific as possible. Simply saying, "I want the argument to end," is too vague. The argument might end, but I'm sure you want more than that, as there was a reason for the argument that you must resolve, and there are also the feelings involved to consider. By setting yourself a clear goal, you can more easily see the steps that need to be taken in order to reach it. This goal should be your ideal vision of resolution while still being realistic and achievable. If you set unrealistic or unachievable goals, you will only be creating further stress for yourself, as when you fail to achieve the goals, you will be frustrated, overwhelmed, and possibly angry. Lastly, you should set a time limit for your goal. Do you want to resolve the conflict today? Tomorrow? If it is a long-term goal, do you hope to have achieved it in a month's time? A year? If you don't set a time limit for your goal, it is easy for time to just pass you by as you continue to make no progress. But, a goal helps you to stay motivated and on track, taking steps as need be. In short, you want your goals to be SMART. This means your goals should be specific, measurable, achievable, relevant, and have a time limit or allocation. Always keep this in mind when practicing problem-solving.

Step Three: Weighing Options and Consequences

Once you know what you want to achieve, it is time to determine how you will go about achieving it. There are various methods you could try, and you might find something that works better for you as an individual. However, the method I recommend for most people is brainstorming. This is a helpful method, as it allows you to think more freely. On an empty page, write down your goal in the center. Give yourself some time to just sit and think without pressure. Around your goal, write out as many ideas as you can think of that could possibly help you achieve your goal. Not all of the ideas have to be completely practical. The point here is to freely think without obstructing yourself. Write down any idea you have. Once you have written down as many resolution ideas as you can think of, you can then worry about making the ideas practical. You can analyze each idea you have written, considering its pros and cons. If an idea isn't completely practical, is there a way you can slightly adjust or change it so that it would work better? Consider all the potential consequences of each option, whether good or bad. As you consider the pros and cons of each idea, narrow down your options to the best two or three.

Step Four: Making Your Decision

Hopefully, brainstorming will make your decision clear. However, you might still be struggling to decide which of the options is best after analyzing them. This could be because you need more information to make a decision, because you are uncertain of your options, or because your goal is unrealistic. If you need more information, then look over the information you already have and see if you are missing something. It could be that you didn't include important information when writing out your problem, creating your goal, or brainstorming solutions. If you still need more information, then determine where you can find it. Can you research online? Can you ask someone for help? Once you gain the information you need, you will likely find it easier to make a decision.

If you are struggling between multiple possible options, then try going over the pros and cons again, and give each option you have a rating between one and ten. You will likely find there is a slight difference in the rating of the two options. For instance, one might be a six, and the other might be a seven. Since the seven scored higher, you can go with that option. You might also try running the options by a friend, asking them for input; this can give you new insight that can help you better determine how to appropriately score and act on the options available. If your goal is unrealistic or unattainable, then no solution you come up with will be enough. Try to break down the problem into multiple steps and solve each step one at a time.

You might also need to rethink your goal. For instance, if your goal is to solve an argument without any hurt feelings, it may not be possible if it is a difficult subject. But, you might be able to change the goal to resolve the argument so that you and the other person come to an understanding. There may still be hurt feelings, but you can work through those in time. Lastly, you might find it helpful to create contingency plans during the brainstorming stage. This can help you feel secure, knowing that even if your plan doesn't work out, you have other options in place ready to act on. For instance, it might look like this:

— If the person won't let me talk, I will: Use breathing exercises to calm down and take notes in a notebook of what I want to say until they give me an opportunity to talk.
— If I become overwhelmed I will: Practice breathing exercises and then calmly explain "I am overwhelmed, can I please have a few moments to collect myself."
— If they say ___ and hurt my feelings I will: I will calm myself down with breathing exercises. I will then write out in a notebook what they said that hurt me, why it hurt me, and the exact emotions I am feeling. I can then calmly explain to them why and how what they said is painful.

By having not only a main plan in place to meet your desired goal but also clear contingency plans written out, you can have confidence going into a difficult situation. This confidence will benefit your cognitive state, making you less prone to anger as you are less likely to feel overwhelmed.

Step Five: Taking Action

After you have a plan in place, you need to make sure you have everything in order to act on it. This might be something you act on immediately for a present problem, such as conflict that has arisen or an immediate problem at work. However, it could also be a long-term plan for a goal; for instance, your goal might be to get a job in a specific field in one year's time.

If the action is long-term or not immediate, then it is often helpful to set visual reminders. You might place post-it notes around that you can see, or you might try writing your goal on a dry erase board somewhere you can easily see it. This is helpful, as people more often complete their goals on time if they have visual reminders.

Step Six: Evaluating the Outcome

Only you can decide whether or not you achieved the goal you set out to accomplish. After you have acted on your goal, when you reach the finish line, whether it is immediate or a year away, take the time to sit down and see how everything turned out. Ask yourself if your goal was realistic, and if you were able to accomplish it. Did you go with your first action option, or did you end up using the contingency plans? How do you feel now it is over? Do you feel proud of your accomplishments, or are you disappointed in anything?

Try to analyze the situation to the best of your ability, writing it down on paper. Try to write down any ways that you succeeded and want to continue doing in the future, along with anything that was unhelpful and you want to change. Write down all your accomplishments step-by-step. You should write the outward accomplishments such as getting the job you desired, using breathing exercises, or having a difficult but necessary conversation.

But, you also want to write down your inward accomplishments, such as staying calm, not getting angry, appreciating your blessings, and experiencing increased joy. While you might not previously have thought of these types of things as accomplishments, they truly are! You have to work hard to change your cognition and improve your mental health, so you should be proud of any of the steps you have taken to do just that. Once you have analyzed the situation, you can better take the information you have gleaned with you in the future to better achieve your goals. You can better appreciate your hard work and success. You can learn from your mistakes. And, you can better see how the problem-solving technique has helped you.

Cognitive Restructuring

As you have learned through the course of this chapter, a person's thoughts—both automatic thoughts and core beliefs—play an integral role in a person's mental well-being and thus their anger management. If you think negatively about a situation or person, you are more likely to become angry. On the other hand, if you rewire your thought process to lessen the negative and increase the positive thoughts, then you are more likely to manage your anger successfully. While it may take consistent hard work at first to manage your anger, you will find it becomes easier over time as these balanced and positive thoughts become your automatic habit over your previous negative thoughts.

The way you can address your negative thoughts, restructuring them into something balanced and healthy, is known as cognitive restructuring. Imagine your mind is a house built out of blocks. While it may be an unbalanced and negative mess at the moment, if you restructure the blocks from the bottom up, then you can build a stronger and more secure structure; this is what cognitive restructuring does to your mind and thought processes.

It allows you to confront your faulty core beliefs, negative automatic thoughts, and cognitive distortions to create something healthier and more balanced than before. Cognitive restructuring is not a single step, but rather a multi-step process. You must put in consistent hard work to see results, but if you follow through, you will see a positive change. Let's look at each step of the cognitive restructuring process in turn, and then you can use the workbook page at the end of this book to try it out for yourself. Use the workbook page any time you find yourself struggling with negative thoughts and anger. You will likely find yourself using the page all the time at first, but you will find as your anger lessens and your cognition becomes more balanced, you will naturally have to use it less frequently.

Step One: Identify Your Distorted Thoughts

It is likely that you are not struggling with a single distorted thought, but many. This is especially true when you first begin cognitive restructuring and have to start working from the bottom up to restructure your cognition. Don't worry; with regular effort and hard work, you will begin to restructure your cognition successfully so that you have fewer distorted thoughts in the future.

For the sake of this exercise, you will use the worksheet and identify a single distorted thought. You will use the worksheet separately for each thought, so you might want to print out multiple copies. Right now, single out a single distorted thought and focus on it alone; you can work on the other thoughts later. As you are now aware, there are ten types of distorted thoughts. In this case, you will be isolating a negative thought and determining whether or not it is a distorted thought, such as "I'm a complete failure."

This thought process can create different emotional reactions in different people. One person might become depressed while another becomes angry at themselves and taking the anger out on those around them. To determine whether or not the thought is a cognitive distortion or a healthy and balanced thought, you will use Socratic questioning. This is a simple list of questions about a given thought that you will find on the workbook page, including:

— Is it realistic?
— Is it based on facts or feelings?
— Is it supported by evidence?
— Could I be misinterpreting the evidence?
— Am I viewing things as black and white or seeing the subtleties?
— Am I thinking this out of habit?

If you ask yourself these questions about the thought example given above, you will find that "I'm a complete failure," is a distorted thought. By first acknowledging that this is distorted thinking, you are now empowered to do something about it.

Step Two: Test Your Thoughts

Once you finish Socratic questioning, you will likely know whether or not your thought is balance, helpful, or healthy. However, in some cases, you may still be unsure. If that is the case, you can move onto testing your thoughts. By putting thought to the test, you can find more evidence either supporting or contradicting the thought. When testing your thought, you want to do it in a safe way that is as controlled as possible. The way this happens will vary depending on what thought you are putting to the test. For example, you may explain the problem and thought to a person you trust and ask for their opinion. It is important that you do this directly rather than passively because if you simply go to Twitter and write a subtweet about your thoughts, you may feel like you are confronting the thought, but you aren't.

You must go to a specific person and have a vulnerable discussion with them. Another way you might test your thoughts is by conducting a safe experiment. For instance, if you believe that you are incapable of learning something, rather than going along with that line of thinking, try setting aside some time to actually try to learn it. If you believe you don't have time for self-care activities, try setting aside fifteen minutes a week to practice a specific self-care exercise. After a few weeks, you can analyze the results. You will likely find that you did have time to practice self-care and that by doing so, you were able to benefit in other areas of your life. If you aren't sure of how you can put a thought to the test safely, try asking someone you trust for advice. Often times, people who are outside of your struggles will have helpful ideas you would not see on your own.

Step Three: Look Over the Evidence

For this step, you will write down the thought you are struggling with. Beneath it, you will write evidence that supports the thought, and in another column, you will write evidence that contradicts the thought. Once you have written out all the available evidence, you can analyze it to see whether the thought is ultimately supported or not. Once you are done analyzing your thought, you will use the available evidence to write a new, more balanced thought. For example, if your previous distorted thought was "I'm a complete failure," your new balanced thought might be, "I made a mistake here, but I also succeeded in other areas. I'm not a failure; I can grow and improve from this experience."

Step Four: Track Your Thinking

If you find yourself regularly struggling with the same line of distorted thinking, no matter what that thought maybe, then it is important to track how frequently you struggle with it. This is because many distorted thoughts simply become habits we think about automatically. The way this happens can vary based on the thought or the person. But, by tracking it, you can more easily address the thought when it occurs. Keep a notebook, journal, or even use the Note app on your phone to track whenever you have the identified distorted thought along with the thought track the time, date, and situation.

This will allow you to see when and why you are struggling with the thought. You might find that you always have the same thought when around a specific person or in a specific situation. Another benefit of tracking the thought is that it makes you intentionally confront it every time it occurs, rather than passively allowing it to damage your cognition. If you confront the thought every time you experience it, you can more easily overcome it and restructure a healthy cognition.

Step Five: Mindfulness

Mindfulness is different from meditation. Rather than attempting to clear your mind, you instead choose to focus on your breathing, the feeling of your muscles moving as the breath enters and leaves your body. You calm your mind focusing on the physical sensations. If your mind begins to wander, it is okay; you can simply gently guide your focus back on your breath. Mindfulness is a wonderful tool both when you are struggling with distorted thoughts and controlling your anger. Although keep in mind that it takes regular practice to achieve the best results. Try practicing mindfulness for a few months several times a day, plus whenever you find yourself struggling with anger or distorted thoughts. You can use the mindfulness exercise from chapter five or find smartphone apps or YouTube videos to guide you through the process.

Step Six: Compassion

Easier said than done is compassion. Whether you are having compassion for others or yourself, it is a struggle. This is especially true if you aren't used to showing compassion. Whether you are used to getting angry at others, yourself, or both—learning to use compassion instead requires a lot of practice. But it is worth it. After struggling with distorted thinking, practice showing compassion, whether to yourself or others. Forgive people for their mistakes. Speak kindly to yourself. Don't hold people to overly difficult standards. Show yourself patience. There are many ways to practice compassion. Everyone deserves compassion. This includes other people and yourself. It may not be easy to sow, but if you regularly put in the effort and practice your CBT exercises, you will find it becomes easier. As you have learned through this chapter, there are many effective cognitive methods to regain control over your anger and bring balance to your cognition. But, it takes daily hard work and practice. Use the workbook pages at the end of this book on a daily basis, consistently doing the work, and you will see improvement.

CHAPTER IV: BEHAVIORAL STRATEGIES

In chapter three, you learned how to use some of the top cognitive methods to improve your mental health and manage your anger. But that is only the tip of the iceberg! In this chapter, we will be focusing on behavioral strategies you can implement on a daily basis to continue progressing toward your goals.

Anger Log

Keeping track of your anger is one important part of managing it. To do this, you can use a notebook, an app on your phone, or the workbook page from the end of this book. It doesn't really matter what you record your anger log in, as long as you include all of the pertinent information. Your anger log should include the trigger, warning signs, response, and the outcome. What does this mean? Well, let's look at two anger log examples, both with the same trigger, but one in which a person doesn't use CBT anger management tools and another where they do use them.

Without CBT Methods:

Date/Time:	*06/05/2021* *7:15pm*
Trigger:	*Significant other dropped my computer and broke it.*
Warning Signs:	*Shaking hands, rushed shallow breathing, face felt hot and flushed, mind felt empty before a sense of rage overcome me.*
Response:	*I screamed at my significant other for breaking my computer. I interrupted their attempts to speak. I stomped over to them and pushed them away from the computer before looking at the damage. I then went to the bedroom, slamming and locking the door.*
Outcome:	*We didn't speak again that night. They slept on the couch. I woke up angry, but then felt guilty when I read a note they left apologizing and saying they ordered me a replacement computer. I know I shouldn't have reacted that way, and now I don't know how to apologize.*

With CBT Methods:

Date/Time:	*06/05/2021*
	7:15pm
Trigger:	*Significant other dropped my computer and broke it.*
Warning Signs:	*Shaking hands, rushed shallow breathing, face felt hot and flushed, mind felt empty before a sense of rage overcome me.*
Response:	*I felt the anger come over me and wanted to yell, but I stopped myself. I closed my eyes, breathed deeply for a few moments, and reminded myself that it was a simple and unintended mistake. I asked them to give me a few moments alone to calm down and assess the damage. After calming myself down further I looked over the damage and assessed it was indeed broken. I used the cognitive restructuring worksheet to balance my thoughts. I then used the problem-solving method to consider potential ways to proceed.*
Outcome:	*Once I calmed down and was no longer angry, I talked with my spouse. They apologized and I forgave them. We discussed problem-solving methods and they offered to replace my computer immediately. I should have the replacement tomorrow, and in the meantime I can use their laptop.* *I am proud of myself for using my coping tools and overcoming my anger. It wasn't easy, but I did well and can see my growth.*

This anger log is great because it allows a person to examine what makes them angry, their warning signs, which helps them calm down, and the outcome. By analyzing the data you build up over time, you can find helpful information. For example, you may find that you have a specific warning sign of coming anger, and by recognizing this warning sign, you can more easily calm yourself down at the first sign of it in the future. You can also see what methods of self-calming work for you and which don't.

You can see your mistakes and how to overcome them in the future. You can also acknowledge and celebrate your successes. Everyone working through anger should keep an anger log, such as this one. Again, you can use the workbook page for your anger log, or you can create one in a notebook or on your phone. Whatever anger tool best for you is great, as long as you include each of the categories included above. Utilize your anger log every time you get angry—never skip using it. If you want to improve, you have to use every opportunity you have to grow and improve. This is one of the most basic steps to anger management with CBT and shouldn't be skimmed over.

Imaginal Anger Exposure

You likely have heard of exposure therapy for people with phobias. For instance, a person with a fear of spiders might undergo exposure therapy to help them feel less afraid around the arachnids. However, most people are unaware of the intricate details of exposure therapy or that it has many uses—one of which is in anger management. Before you get into potentially-angering situations for anger exposure therapy, it is important to start small. Most people are unaware, but the first step of exposure therapy is imaginal exposure. This means you create an exposure scenario and play it through in your mind's eye, imagining in detail how it would play out. You might just be astonished at how effective this can be! For best results, practice imaginal exposure therapy regularly. I recommend practicing for at least ten minutes three times a week, but if you can practice a few minutes each day, it is even better. There is a workbook page at the end of the book that you can use to help walk you through imaginal exposure therapy. But, for now, let's examine how it might play out. First, you would write down a potentially angering situation.

For example, in the situation category, you might write down that the angering situation is a person cutting you off in traffic. This should include the indisputable facts of the situation. In the interpretation category, you should write down your interpretation of the events. While the previous section focused on the facts of the situation, this should focus on how you feel about the situation—the emotions, your thoughts, beliefs, and why you feel angry. Next, you should rate how angry this situation makes you form a scale of 0 to 100. You want to create a variety of situations such as this at different anger scales. Some might only be a 25 on the anger scale, but later on, you might be able to work up to a 90 on the anger scale. In the last column, you should write out the coping mechanisms you can use. This will vary depending on the situation. For instance, if you have time and are in an area that allows, you might be able to pull off the side of the road to close your eyes and practice mindfulness exercises. But, even if you can't do that, you can still practice deep breathing while you drive, recite positive affirmations, utilize Socratic questioning to restructure your thought and imagine a calming environment such as a garden with a small fish pond.

Once you fill out the worksheet with the above information, try to close your eyes and imagine everything in detail. Imagine the car cutting you off, the surge of adrenaline and the following anger, the harsh words you might think or even yell, the honking of your horn, and the speed of the car. Imagine exactly what you would think and feel in this situation, allowing yourself to actually feel the emotions and anger wash over you. Follow it up by imagining yourself work through the anger with your anger management techniques. Actually, practice your Socratic questioning and deep breathing—not just imagining it, but actually doing it. Allow yourself to become fully immersed in the imaginary experience so that it feels real. Once you are done and have calmed down the emotions, then congratulate yourself! You just practiced imaginal exposure therapy. It can be tiring because you are allowing yourself to actually experience the anger and accompanying emotions. But, by doing this regularly, you can learn to actively practice your management exercise and how to overcome the anger. Practice this exercise with the created situation regularly until you find it no longer makes you angry.

Once you master this experience, you can create a new experience on the worksheet that is a greater anger difficulty and continue to practice that experience. By practicing imaginal exposure therapy regularly, you will find that when you actually experience situations that make you angry, you are more prepared to overcome them. It will make real-life situations easier to deal with, helping you to react with self-control and temperance rather than with volatile anger.

In Vivo Anger Exposure

After a person masters imaginal anger exposure, they can proceed to in vivo anger exposure. With the in vivo method, rather than imagining a scenario, a person actually begins to dip their toes into a situation—fully in the present without having to imagine the scenario. This is the form of exposure therapy that most people are familiar with. When you imagine this form of exposure therapy, you might picture a therapist walking their patient with a phobia through interacting with the said phobia, whether it be heights, spiders, or any number of other phobias. But, rather than using it for phobias, you can use it for anger management. The reason for this is because anger is closely tied to anxiety and stress. Many people may become stressed by a situation, and that stress gives rise to anger. But, if you practice exposure therapy, you can potentially lessen the anger and improve your handling of the situation. In order to practice exposure therapy, you first must learn how to practice various methods of calming the mind and body; this can include breathing techniques, meditation, mindfulness, and other practices. It is vital that you have to tools to calm yourself before attempting to expose yourself to stressful situations. Otherwise, you won't be able to appropriately handle the situation. This means you should regularly practice the other methods and worksheets in this book before moving onto this step. When you practice exposure therapy, you should have four goals:

— Analyze triggers
— Reduce anger arousal
— Response prevention
— Inspire hope

These are important steps. By analyzing your triggers, you can understand how and why they affect you, preparing you to better handle triggers in the future when they are outside of your control. By reducing your anger arousal, you directly reduce the amount of anger you feel in a given situation; the anger may not go away completely. But, by lessening it through consistent hard work, you can make it easier to manage.

With response prevention, you teach yourself tools to react to any anger you are experiencing less. Instead of responding to the anger by yelling, throwing things, or other destructive behaviors, you can learn to implement helpful anger management tools. Lastly, by implementing exposure therapy, you can inspire hope in yourself. This happens when you successfully implement exposure therapy and gain confidence in your ability to handle a situation. You will see that with regular hard work, you can achieve your goals, lessen your anger, and manage any anger you do experience better. This hope will encourage you to continue growing by putting in more effort. Keep in mind that the steps we are about to outline are meant to be completed over a period of weeks, not days. It takes time to build up your ability to cope with a situation and utilize your management tools. You can't simply jump into the deep end. Start with wading into exposure therapy, and before you know it, you will be "swimming" like a pro! This entire process would usually take about nine months with a CBT-trained therapist, so it should take the same amount of time (if not longer) if you are working on it alone.

Step One

Create a list of your anger triggers and a list of your anger management tools. This list must be customized for each person, so what yours looks like will be different, but let's look at an example.

Anger Triggers:	Management Tools:
Being ignored	*Deep breathing*
Being lied to	*Positive affirmations*
Being yelled at	*Cognitive restructuring*
Being disrespected	*Meditation*
Being interrupted	*Mindfulness*
Personal space intrusion	*Calming music*
Being put in danger	*Stress ball*
Insults	*Exercise*

This list allows you to better understand yourself. Don't feel like you have to create it all at once. You should take your time to ensure you fill it out accurately and extensively. Take a few days, or even a week or two, and whenever you think of an anger trigger or a management tool that helps, write it down. By understanding your anger triggers, you know where to begin addressing problems. You also know when to expect your anger to surge, meaning you can be prepared to address the anger with your management tools. Having a list of management tools gives you hope, as you can see the many possibilities. Even if one tool on its own isn't enough, you can combine the use of two or three to help calm any anger you may experience. Rather than focusing on the negative, such as the mistakes you have made through your anger, focus on the positive. This doesn't mean you ignore your mistakes, but that you see them in a more balanced light while also acknowledging the positive.

For instance, you may have previously thought, "I made such a mistake; I am a failure!" But, now you can choose to frame it in the more positive light of, "I made a mistake when I gave into my anger, but I now know how I can grow. I can address these struggles by using these specific tools, and with effort, I know I will make progress! I can grow and improve; I have all the tools and motivation I need to succeed!" See the difference? The second one doesn't ignore mistakes made, but it focuses on how you can grow and improve from where you are now.

Step Two.

 Practice reliving a real-life experience that made you angry. It could be when a person cuts you off in traffic when someone degraded you, or any number of other situations. Find something that still affects you emotionally when you think about it, so it will most likely be something recent. To relive this memory, tell the story aloud. You could tell the story to a person you trust and who has consisted of helping you, or you can simply tell yourself the story while looking in a mirror. While you tell the story, allow yourself to feel the emotions without stopping the story. Ride the wave of the experience.

If you begin to feel yourself getting angry, calm yourself down with one or several of your anger management methods—such as deep breathing or mindfulness. When you are done reliving the experience, ask yourself why it made you angry, your feelings about it, what you were thinking, and what/if there is anything you could have done differently to improve the situation. If you had to rate how angry the experience made you between 0-100, how would you rate it? Practice this exercise regularly, ideally practicing it with different anger-inducing experiences. One day you might practice a situation that made you angry with a stranger, and another day you might practice one where you got angry at a friend. It is helpful to practice as many different situations as possible.

Step Three.

Thinking back over situations that have made you angry in the past, practice using the cognitive restructuring worksheet. Once you are done filling out the sheet, try reading aloud all of your answers. It is helpful to read it aloud to another person, but again, you can simply read it to yourself in the mirror, as well. This is helpful, as you will notice, you experience the emotions more deeply and absorb the message more strongly when you read it aloud rather than silently.

By reading aloud your cognitive restructuring worksheet, you will absorb the more balanced healthy thoughts at a deeper level, which is what you want. Again, practice this with a variety of situations throughout the week. Keep in mind; sometimes, anger is the correct response. If someone is pushing your boundaries, sometimes a strong word or a slightly raised voice is needed.

For instance, if someone keeps putting their hand on you and you have asked them to stop, yet they continue, you can stretch your arm out to create distance (without touching them or acting violently) and slightly raise your voice with a firm, "I said stop!" We all have boundaries, and they are important. Yet, some people insist on pushing these boundaries. The vital lesson is how to stand up to such a person without allowing your anger to get the best of you. It is all about balance. If you begin struggling with anger at any time in the process, remember to practice your calming exercises! This is a vital step, as you should be learning to implement these tools to manage your anger. If you don't use the tools, then you will only be reinforcing the bad habit of allowing your anger to take over. Practice these tools regularly throughout the day, even when you are not working through exposure therapy. You want to build up your brain "muscles" of using these tools throughout the day so that they are ready when you need them.

Step Four.

Once you have learned to explain situations that make you angry while using your management tools to stay calm, you can move onto more difficult exposure. This exposure is more direct. But, before you begin, you should start with a few minutes of calming exercises, such as mindfulness and deep breathing.

After you are done, you can move onto the exposure therapy. At this point, if you were working with a therapist, they would begin to directly expose you to situations that make you angry. Keep in mind this is done in a controlled environment with the client's full consent. If the client wants to stop at any point, the therapist will stop. But, to expose the client to a difficult situation, the therapist may begin to use phrases that would make the client angry. For instance, they may call them insults, deride them, bump into them, or generally be rude. Again, this is only done with the client's consent, and a therapist should never do this without their consent. This must be done very carefully.

During this process, the client practices their calming techniques and conflict de-escalation. For example, they might practice what the client can do if a person starts screaming at them. Rather than getting angry and screaming back, they can practice using de-escalation techniques by asking the therapist to stop screaming, explaining how it makes them feel, and talking calmly and rationally. This allows the person to develop a direct real-life experience. The exposure therapy session then ends with a five-minute deep breathing and mindfulness exercise to help calm the mind and body. This exercise can be done in stages based on their intensity. For instance, the client can rate how difficult certain circumstances are from 0-100, and they can work with the least difficult exposures first, gradually building up to the more difficult exposures. This process of exposure therapy continues until the patient can stay calm in all situations, handling them in a healthy, helpful, and balanced way without anger. Sometimes, a therapist will bring in additional people to help with exposure therapy.

A neutral third-party or even a friend of yours who has consented to help may come in to play the role of the "bad guy" in the exposure scenario. In other cases, such as with kids who become aggressive and prone to bullying, the therapist might have multiple kids role-playing through an exposure scenario together. Or, a married couple might practice an exposure scenario, such as replaying an argument they have had in the past.

All of this is done with the strict supervision of the therapist, who can make sure things are done in a productive, safe, and healthy way, and that no boundaries are crossed.

Remember, this therapy usually takes approximately nine weeks. This is because anger has become a habit, and it is a difficult habit to break. Exposure therapy is not an easy therapeutic method, but it can be an effective one when used correctly.

Assertion Training

It is easy to think that because you want to reduce and manage your anger that you can't stand your ground or against those who might wish to wrong you, but that is not the case! In fact, assertion training is a great aspect of anger management with CBT. With this training method, you can learn how to stand up for yourself or others regarding your needs, boundaries, and beliefs. It allows you to calmly and directly communicate your point with diplomacy. If a person lacks assertiveness, it will likely show itself in a few ways, such as:

— Passive behavior, complying with others.
— Difficulty standing up for beliefs, rights, or boundaries.

— Difficulty communicating their point of view.

Assertion training is important because it allows a person to learn how to stand up for themselves or others without relying on anger. Too often, people rely on anger to demand their boundaries be respected when there are better ways you can handle the situation without anger. Not only that, but some people may lack assertion and passively comply with others, only to later become angry because they were taken advantage of. With assertion training, you can avoid both of these problems.

Assertion training allows you to overcome the mistakes of both passive and aggressive behavior. With passive behavior, you sacrifice your own needs or the needs of those around you in favor of a third party. With aggressive behavior, you sacrifice the needs of others in favor of your own needs. Neither of these options is helpful or balanced.

But, assertiveness allows you to learn the needs and find a balance between the needs of everyone. It allows you to state your needs, or the needs of those with you, and find a compromise to a problem that works best for everyone. You will likely find that your assertiveness will change over the course of your lifetime. This is because we are always changing. Sometimes this change will be positive, and sometimes we must make mistakes before righting ourselves. This is why sometimes people lose their assertiveness when they try to reign in their aggression because they confuse the two. But, ideally, it would be easier for a person to learn to lessen their aggression without also lessening their assertiveness.

Thankfully, even if you find you are not assertive enough, you can improve it with this assertion training. To determine your personal assertiveness, try taking this short quiz. When taking the quiz, try to answer as honestly as possible. To do this, you have to view yourself accurately, which can be hard, but it is an important skill to develop. For each item that accurately represents you, write a checkmark. At the end of the quiz, count how many items you checked off. If you scored above a five, you likely need to work on your assertiveness with assertion training.

Assertiveness Quiz	
Do you struggle to tell people what you think?	
Do you struggle to freely show your emotions?	
Do you struggle to ask others for help?	
Are you socially shy?	
Do you struggle to say something if someone pushes your boundaries?	
Do you struggle to tell people "no?"	
Do you struggle to return items that are broken or not as described to the store?	
Do you struggle to say something if someone interrupts you?	
Do you struggle to say something if someone says something unfair against you?	
Do you struggle to have self-confidence in your decision making?	
Do you allow others to push their work onto you?	
Do you say "sorry" frequently, even for no reason?	
Are you frequently self-deprecating?	
Do you only give positive feedback?	
Are you always trying to prove yourself?	
Score:	

While you may believe passive actions such as those in the quiz are neutral or even positive, that is not the case. When you are overly passive, you allow people to harm you or even those around you—which is not healthy or helpful. It is important to learn how to stand up for yourself and what you believe to be right. This does not mean you have to be aggressive and angry. It doesn't mean you have to prioritize yourself over others. It simply means that you see you are just as important as other people, and your feelings and how people treat you matter, too. If that is not enough to convince you that assertiveness is important, keep in mind that people tend to struggle when interacting with someone who is passive. People often find those who are "pushovers" difficult to interact with. They might initially feel bad for the person for being so passive, but eventually, they might get tired of overly passive actions. This is because when you are overly passive, it negatively affects those around you. If you want the best for yourself and those you care about, it is important to find balance. You can become assertive while still caring for others and without being aggressive or angry. If you struggle to see the difference between being assertive and aggressive, take a look at these lists describing the two behaviors. It might help to clear up any misunderstandings you have of these actions in practice.

Assertive Behaviors:	Aggressive Behaviors:
You request your desires or needs	*You focus on your own needs while disregarding those of other people*
You respect yourself and others	
You listen to what others need	*You must always be the one to "win" and anything other than getting your way is a "failure"*
You say what you think or feel clearly	
You stand up for what's right	*You will raise your voice, bully, or force people to get your way.*
You maintain healthy boundaries	
You look for win-win situations in life	*You don't listen to negative feedback*

As I hope you can see from the above lists, assertiveness and aggressiveness are completely different behaviors. You can be assertive without being angry and aggressive, and just because you are attempting to lessen your anger doesn't mean you have to lose your assertiveness. Now, let's look at some steps you can take to develop your assertion.

Step One

When having a conversation with a person—especially a difficult conversation—it is important that you show that you are actively listening and understanding what they say. People understandably feel negatively when a person doesn't listen to what they have to say. To achieve a helpful and balanced solution, both you and they need to be genuinely listened to. While you may think you have been listening to a person, often times when in a conversation, we focus on what we need to say and how we will reply. Instead, your focus should be on what they are saying as they are saying it.

Once they are done, you can worry about what you will say. If you have any confusion about what they have said, you can ask genuine and pertinent questions to clear up the misunderstanding. This is better than doing nothing because if you are silent about your misunderstandings, it can cause problems later. Some tips to show you are actively listening include:

— Make eye contact while speaking.
— Don't interrupt.
— Notice a person's non-verbal communication, such as tone of voice, facial expressions, and body language.
— Listen without jumping to conclusions or judging.
— Listen without worrying about what you will say next.
— Ask pertinent and helpful questions.
— Don't impose your thoughts or solutions.

— Try paraphrasing what they have said when it is your turn to speak; this shows you are listening and can help them hear what you believe they said so that if there was a miscommunication, they could clear it up.
— Stay focused on what they are saying without becoming distracted.

Keep in mind that this list is for the average neurotypical person. If someone is neuroatypical and has a condition such as autism or ADHD, then one or more of these items listed may not be possible. For instance, they may struggle to look a person in the eye, or they might struggle to stay focused and need the help of a fidget device to listen. But, even if you are neuroatypical and can't follow one or two of the listed items, that is okay! You can always follow the other suggestions, and you can even explain to a person the situation. Saying something such as "I am listening to you, but it helps me focus on what you say if I use a fidget device.

Thanks for understanding," or "please trust that I'm listening, but I struggle to look people in the eye, so while we talk I'll be looking [another place,] so please know that I am focusing." Simply put, whether you are neurotypical or neuroatypical, you can show a person that you are listening. All it takes is following a few steps and communicating any specific needs.

Step Two

In this step, you are focusing on saying your thoughts and feelings. It can be difficult to do this, as you might be feeling strong emotions, such as anger, sadness, inadequacy, or any number of other feelings depending on the situation. But, learning to master this process can greatly improve your relationships, communication, and of course, assertiveness. You want to say how you think or feel without judgment or blame.

It is also important that you address what a person said, rather than blowing past it straight to what you want to communicate. For instance, if you and someone else are struggling because you both said something hurtful to the other, you might say: *"I can see how you feel. I'm sorry I hurt you when I said that; I will work to improve in that area. However, when you [said or did] that, it made me feel [hurt] because [reasons.] I would appreciate it if we could find a solution that meets both of our needs."*

Step Three

In the final step, you learn to express your needs and desires. This is something both parties should do so that you both understand the needs of the other and can work to find a solution. For instance, you might say, *"I really need this task done by a certain time due to [reasons,] but I understand that might be difficult to accomplish. Is there any way we can work together to meet the deadline while also meeting any needs you have?"*

By learning to actively listen, express your thoughts and emotions, and express any needs you might have, you can learn how to implement assertion when necessary. There are many places in life that these steps can help you. Even when these steps are not applicable, you will find that by learning assertion through this process, you can take the lessons you learned in assertion to other areas of life.

Time-Out

When you are in a difficult situation—especially if you are angry—it is easy to believe that you have to stay in the situation. That you have to keep pushing to be heard. That you have to keep fighting for what you want. That you have to stick through it until there is a resolution. However, I have a secret to tell you: you *don't* have to. You can take a step back. You can take a break or a time-out.

While not always possible, in many situations, you can take a step back to calm down. This is something that anyone should practice when they feel the need to, but especially those with anger issues. After all, it is better to take a few minutes to calm yourself or think a situation through rather than losing control of your temper. Whether you are in an argument with someone or another high-stress situation, if you are struggling to keep your cool or need time to think through an issue, simply be honest with the person you're with. Say, "I am becoming overwhelmed, and I need just a few minutes. Please excuse me; I will be right back." By saying this, the person knows that if you leave, it is not because you are blowing them off.

They also know to expect your return shortly. Not only will this benefit you, but it will also benefit them as if you become overwhelmed or angry, it only causes problems for everyone. After you leave, you can take a moment to calm yourself by using deep breathing or mindfulness. You might also spend some time with a problem-solving, cognitive restructuring, or a faulty thinking worksheet (from the end of this book) to help you work through your thoughts and emotions.

This will allow you to come back to the person more capable of holding a productive conversation. It is easy to tell ourselves that we shouldn't take a time-out because it feels selfish or because we feel we have to keep fighting until we get our way, but that is not true. A short time-out is often the best solution for everyone involved. You may find yourself having to use time-outs frequently at first, and that's okay. In time, as you practice and become better at anger management, you will likely need them less and less.

CHAPTER V: EMOTIONAL AND PHYSIOLOGICAL TECHNIQUES

In this chapter, we will be going over-emotional and physiological techniques you can use to calm your body and mind. These are great to use whenever you feel your anger rising, whether you feel the emotion itself or tell-tale warning signs such as shaking or increased heart rate. By taking just a few moments to practice these techniques, you can calm your body and mind, allowing you to better manage your anger and stay in control.

These techniques work best if you practice them regularly. It is generally recommended that you practice these on a daily basis at times when you are not angry, plus any time you feel the need to calm down. By practicing these at times when you are already calm, such as when you wake up in the morning or on your lunch break, your body and mind will learn to better react and relax when you need these tools the most. For instance, imagine listening to a calming song.

If the song is new to you and you play it to try to calm down when angry, it likely won't help very much. However, if you train your body to use the song when you are already calm, then if you listen to the same song when you need to calm down, your body and brain will already associate it with the feeling of relaxation, thus improving its effect. Using these techniques is much like training a muscle. Only by training using them regularly will you strengthen your body and mind and experience their true effects.

I recommend scheduling time for these activities every day, not counting on your ability to remember to complete them. You have to make time and stick to it. Add these techniques to a daily to-do list or set reminders on your phone. Either way, it is important that you take the time if you truly want to see improvement in your mental well-being and learn to manage your anger.

Mindfulness

Often times, people confuse mindfulness and meditation when the two are completely separate techniques. We will go into meditation later, but for now, let's have a look at mindfulness. This is a great technique for anyone to use, whether they are complete beginners to the technique or have years of practice.

Simply put, mindfulness is the practice of focusing on your present state of being. This means you take the time to slow down and appreciate the breath in your lungs, the way your muscles move as you breathe, and how you feel. Mindfulness gives you the chance to become attuned to what is going on in your body. By doing this, you can calm both mind and body, giving you the chance to act intentionally rather than simply reacting.

You can easily practice mindfulness no matter where you are. You can choose to practice it before you get out of bed in the morning, on your lunch break, in a parked car, or you can even excuse yourself to the restroom and practice there if nowhere else is available. You don't need any tools to practice mindfulness; all you need is a minute or two of time. Try to practice mindfulness at least once a day at a scheduled time, such as before you leave for work in the morning. You can practice it additionally whenever you find your stress levels rising or when you begin to notice anger warning signs. It is important to understand that your mind will wander at times when practicing mindfulness—especially if your emotions are running high. It's okay and natural! You shouldn't chastise yourself or become stressed if your mind wanders, as it is simply a part of mindfulness.

Whenever you find your mind wandering from your calm focus, you simply have to gently guide your focus back and away from your worries. This may seem discouraging to some people at first, but it is actually a great opportunity. This gives you the chance to teach your mind to turn away from worries and toward your mindful focus. By practicing this regularly, you will find it becomes easier to regain focus when you are in an emotionally difficult situation. You are exercising those brain muscles, which is always a great thing! Don't judge yourself or become worried if you have trouble focusing; simply do your best, and you will find it becomes easier in time.

Now, let's look at the step-by-step process of practicing mindfulness:

1. Find a quiet and calm location where you can sit or lay down comfortably.

This will vary based on the person—one person may prefer to sit with their legs crossed, another may choose to sit straight in a chair with their hands resting on their thighs, and yet another may find that laying down is best. Whatever option you choose, you want to be able to comfortably stay in that position for the duration of the mindfulness exercise.

You may not be able to sit or lay in your preferred method in all circumstances, but find what is most comfortable in your given situation/location.

2. Decide on a time for your mindfulness exercise.

It is often helpful to set a timer on your phone for your desired time, but if you don't have a clock or a timer, you can just wing it. I suggest starting with a short time in the beginning, between two and five minutes. Over time, you can increase the time period up to ten or even fifteen minutes. Sometimes you may only have time for one or two minutes of mindfulness, and that's okay. Even a minute of mindfulness can help calm the mind.

3. Close your eyes and bring your attention to your body.

Feel your breath enter and leave your lungs. Notice how the air feels entering and leaving your nostrils, the way your chest rises and falls, the way your stomach expands and contracts. Notice how your breathing feels through your whole body, focusing on the slightest of sensations.

4. Your mind may begin to wander, and that's okay.

With kindness and without judgment, simply bring your attention back to the sensation of your breathing. You will likely have to do this multiple times through the mindfulness exercise, and that's okay. It's simply a part of the process.

Continue until your given set time is complete or you feel relaxed in both body and mind.

Mindful Exercise

Exercise can be a great way to calm the body and mind and manage anger. This is especially true when you combine the mindfulness technique with it to create a mindful exercise routine. Whatever method of exercise you prefer—whether it be swimming, running, weight lifting, or even dancing—you can incorporate mindfulness into your routine. It is a wonderful opportunity to practice mindfulness while your blood is pumping harder, your muscles are moving, and you get to experience syncing your mind and body for relaxation.

The steps are simple and adaptable to any form of exercise; let's have a look:

1. As you are preparing to start your exercise session, remain mindful of your purpose—that you will be exercising with a purpose. That you will be focusing on your breath and the sensation of your muscles. That you will feel the air and sunlight on your skin. The way your body moves. That every movement you make will be intentional and with focus on the sensation of the motion.

2. Begin by warming up for five minutes with gentle motions. Stretches are often a good choice. As you do your warm-up, focus on matching your rate of breathing to your movement. You want your breath and movement to be in sync and rhythmic. This will allow your entire body and mind to balance together through the exercise.

3. After warming up, start your exercise of choice, starting out gently and gradually increasing the intensity. As you exercise, continue to focus on matching your breathing to your movements. Focus on and deeply feel the movement of your muscles and breath.

4. Near the end of your exercise, try increasing the intensity or speed. Feel the push and pull of your muscles, your lungs working harder to get in more oxygen. Your body is alive and alert; allow yourself to fully focus on that experience.

5. Begin to slow down the intensity slowly, gradually increasing your pace over about five minutes until you stop. During this process, continue synchronizing your breathing to your movement and focusing on the sensation.

6. Allow yourself to sit and rest for a few minutes. While your breathing slows and your muscles begin to relax, allow your eyes to close and focus on the sensation of your heartbeat slowing, your breathing becoming easier, and the tired ache in your muscles. Notice how alive and awake you feel.

Meditation

There are many forms of meditation, each with its own benefits. I will be teaching you how to practice mantra mediation, but you can also find YouTube videos and smartphone apps that walk you through guided mediation, metta meditation, vipassana mediation, unguided mediation, and more. There are countless free resources out there that make meditation simple, and I recommend putting them to use!

Mantra meditation is a simple method that you can complete on your own simply by following a series of steps. It is also a great method for anger management, as you can use different mantras based on your needs at any given time.

Just like with mindfulness, meditation is something you should practice daily. I recommend practicing one session of meditation every day, plus any additional sessions when you are feeling stress or anger and could benefit from the balance.

Let's get started:

1. Before you begin your meditation session, you need to choose the mantra you will use. You don't always have to use the same mantra. In fact, it can be helpful to choose the mantra depending on how you feel. If you are feeling angry, then use a mantra that targets the anger, and the same is true if you are feeling stressed sad, or any other difficult emotions.

2. You want a mantra that you can focus on for a positive effect. Just as you focus on your breathing when practicing mindfulness, you will be focusing on your mantra during your meditation. You can choose a simple one-word mantra, such as "peace" or "forgiveness. But you can also choose short phrases. Some mantra options for anger include "let it go," "peace is in reach," "it is what it is," "I forgive myself," "I can do this," "this shall pass," "my inner peace can't be disturbed," "I prosper on love," or "breathe in the peace, exhale the negative."

3. Find a quiet and calm location where you can sit or lay down comfortably. This will vary based on the person—one person may prefer to sit with their legs crossed, another may choose to sit straight in a chair with their hands resting on their thighs, and yet another may find that laying down is best. Whatever option you choose, you want to be able to comfortably stay in that position for the duration of the meditation session.

4. You may not be able to sit or lay in your preferred method in all circumstances, but find what is most comfortable in your given situation/location.

5. Allow your eyes to close and clear your body and mind with a few regular breaths breathed in through your nose and out through your mouth. After three or five breaths, close your mouth and breathe normally through your nose at a relaxed pace.

6. Silently repeat your chosen mantra in your mind. This should be done relaxed and slowly. It may naturally be timed with your breath or not; either option is okay; go with whichever option feels comfortable. You want the silent inner representation of the mantra to be easy and effortless, almost as if you were hearing it be spoken rather than repeating it yourself.

7. Eventually, you will find that your mind begins to wander. This is normal. It is nothing to be stressed or disappointed about; there is no judgment in this as it is simply a part of the process. It doesn't mean you are doing meditation "wrong," as it is something that happens with everyone who meditates. Don't worry about trying to empty your mind; that is not the purpose of this meditation. Instead, whenever you notice that your mind has wandered, gently guide it away from your thoughts and back to your mantra.

8. The length of time you meditate will vary from person to person. When you first begin meditating, try to aim for five to seven minutes. The intermediate level would be fifteen to twenty minutes, and advanced is thirty or more minutes. Don't feel discouraged if you can

only meditate for short periods at a time at first; that is completely normal! Your brain is like a muscle, and you need to regularly exercise that muscle to work up to increased time lengths. Try to use a timer when you meditate so that you can know when your set time period is up without getting distracted watching the clock. Often times, a cell phone timer works well.

9. When you are done with your set meditation time, continue to keep your eyes closed for one to two minutes as you allow your mind to begin to wander again without using your mantra. This allows you to slowly bring your mind back to your present. Open your eyes, and you are done!

Deep Breathing

Also known as diaphragm breathing, deep breathing is a common technique used to calm both the mind and body. This is not only because it helps your mind become attuned to your body but also because it prompts actual physical changes in the body, such as the release of calming hormones. By practicing deep breathing regularly, you can find it easier to release stress, let go of anger, and find peace. I recommend practicing deep breathing exercises three times a day when you are in a neutral emotional state, plus whenever you are struggling with your emotions. This means if you have a tough day, you might practice your standard three sessions of breathing exercises plus an additional three or four when you are trying to calm down from anger and stress.

I recommend practicing your three standard sessions of deep breathing, one each in the morning, afternoon, and evening so that you experience the benefits all throughout the day. When practicing these sessions, it is ideal if you can find a comfortable place to sit or lay on your back. But, when you are in a pinch and need to practice deep breathing to calm down, you can simply practice it while standing. Deep breathing is simple; try following these steps:

1. Ideally, find a comfortable place to sit or stand. You can sit in a chair with your feet on the ground, sit with your legs crossed on the floor, or you can lay down on your back with your posture straight.

2. If you choose to lay down, keep a pillow under your head so that your diaphragm isn't at an awkward angle. For comfort, you can also bend your legs or place a pillow under your knees.

If you are sitting, keep your posture upright but with your muscles relaxed. This will give you a good posture to avoid slouching without being overly stiff or uncomfortable.

3. Place one hand on your chest directly below your sternum and the other palm-flat on your abdomen directly above your belly button. This will allow you to focus on how the diaphragm moves your stomach in and out.

4. Now, slowly breathe in deeply through your nose. When you do this, you should breathe deeply enough so that your stomach extends on its own, moving your hand with it. This should happen without you intentionally pushing your abdomen muscles, as that defeats the purpose. The movement and airflow should all feel natural and smooth.

As you breathe in this way, the palm you have resting on your chest should not move much.

5. Purse your lips and slowly allow your breath to release through your mouth. Don't rush the breath's release; it should be slow and steady, taking five or more seconds to release. Your abdomen and hand should relax inward as you exhale.

Ideally, you want to practice at least three inhales/exhales of deep breathing at a time. However, ideally, you can increase the amount of time you practice deep breathing, aiming for anywhere between three to ten minutes.

Relaxation

There are many techniques for relaxation in CBT, as it is a common problem that people with a variety of struggles can experience. Whether you have anxiety, depression, anger, insomnia, addiction, or any number of struggles, relaxation techniques can help you reach your goals. By using relaxation techniques, you can calm your mind, reduce your urges, and more easily act with wisdom and temperance. Whenever you find yourself struggling with maladaptive thoughts or urges, then calm yourself with a relaxation technique before doing anything else.

When using relaxation techniques, it is important to keep in mind that there are many different ones you can use with CBT. No one technique is better than the others. But, you will likely find that some techniques are more helpful for you personally than other techniques. If one technique doesn't work for you, that's okay; you can keep trying until you find one that does work. Lastly, keep in mind that some relaxation techniques only become effective when you have built the habit up in your daily life.

For Progressive Muscle Relaxation:

— If possible, sit or lay in a comfortable position with your eyes closed. Attempt to relax your muscles.

— While your body is relaxed, clench your fists and focus on the sensation of your muscles and skin tightening. Hold this for a few moments feeling the slight discomfort. When your hands begin to feel uncomfortable, release your fists, and experience the sensation of your muscles in your hands returning to normal.

— In the same way, now clench your feet and curl your toes tight. Allow yourself to feel the sensation in the same way before again releasing the muscles.

— Gradually work through muscles in your body, tightening and relaxing them in turn.

CHAPTER VI: WHAT AN ANGER-FREE LIFE REQUIRES

In this final chapter on living anger-free, we will be looking over how the implementation of diet, time management, goals, and more, can help you to attain your anger-free life. This is not all something you can expect to happen at once—it takes time to create structure and learn to control your anger—but with consistent effort and hard work, you can attain the anger-free life you seek.

Time Management

While time management might not at first appear to be a part of anger management, that is not the case! The truth is that if you don't manage your time well, you will be unable to incorporate your anger management techniques into your life as you should. The result is that you will fail to accomplish your techniques as you should, and your anger will suffer the consequences, all because time management wasn't implemented. As if that weren't enough, if you have poor time management, you will struggle to finish other tasks you need to complete, and the stress of that knowledge will likely push your anger over the edge. Yet, you don't need to worry. With the help of time management, you can complete your tasks, and you can incorporate your anger management techniques. I am here to help and give you the tool you need. All you have to do is take the initiative and continuously put in the effort to practice good time management. It may be easier said than done, but it is more than possible. In general, people have five or six areas of their lives that their time is divided between. This includes:

— Home time – when you spend time working around the house and yard.
— Work/school time – when you are at or on your way to work/school.
— Me time – when you practice self-care, sleep, eat, or practice hobbies.
— Other time – when you spend time with family and friends.
— Quiet time – when you spend time quietly with your thoughts, such as with meditation, deep breathing, or mindfulness.
— Us time – if you are in a relationship, this is when you spend one-on-one time with your significant other.

In order to manage your time, you need to know roughly how much time you devote to each of these categories each week. For instance, whether you go to work/school twenty or forty hours a week will greatly vary how much time you have for everything else. Whether you have a significant other will change whether or not you have "us" time. Try writing out a list of what your typical week looks like and how many hours you devote to each category of time.

After you finish writing out your time, consider if there are any areas of your life you would like to add more time to, areas you would prefer to scale back, whether you have been including unnecessary time-wasters, and any other changes you would like to make to how you spend a week. Remember, if you want to add more time to one area, such as me time, then you need to find another area or two that it can come out of. It may take some time to complete this overview, so don't feel like you have to complete it all at once. You can take a rest and come back to complete it another day if you are busy.

To improve your daily time management, I recommend using a daily planner that includes monthly and daily pages, and optionally weekly, as well. This is beneficial, as you can easily view your month and any plans you have scheduled at a glance. In the daily section, you can write down your to-do list. You should use this to-do list every day to ensure you complete all of your needed tasks, including your anger management tools such as meditation and deep breathing.

Optionally, you can use a regular yearly calendar and create a to-do list on a plain sheet of paper every day. This option is inexpensive, and you don't have to worry about running out of space for your to-do list. If your page gets filled up, you can just flip it over and write more or grab another blank page. When creating your to-do list, you want to make it as detailed as possible; for instance, it might look like this:

— Eat 3 healthy/balanced meals
— Work from 8am-5pm
— Deep breathing x3
— Meditation – 5 minutes
— Mindful exercise – 30 minutes
— Run by the grocery store
— Cook dinner
— Skincare
— Call and make an appointment with ____
— Make tomorrow's to-do list
— Print out extra cognitive restructuring worksheets

As you can see, this list includes both small and big tasks that a person might have to accomplish. By doing this, you can make sure you don't forget anything important. Your anger management exercises should always be on this list, as they are an important priority that you don't want to forget or neglect.

Goal Setting

If you hope to get somewhere, you need a goal. Otherwise, you will be running without direction and just hoping you end up somewhere nice. But, the truth is, if you don't have a goal to work toward, you might not like where you end up. The good news is that setting up goals is simple if you use the SMART method. When you create SMART goals, it means that they are Specific, Measurable, Attainable, Realistic, and Time-limited. Ideally, you will create both long-term and short-term SMART goals.

The best way to do this is to look at where you want to be in a year from now, keeping the SMART tenants in mind. Create a goal for a specific date in one year. Once you have created your long-term goal, you can then look at what's steps you need to take to get there and create short-term goals using those steps. For example, let's look at time long-term anger management goals:

— Learn to notice the warning signs of anger and find alternative healthy ways to express, ease, and resolve the feelings.
— Learn to manage my feelings of excessive anger and rage.
— Practice my anger management skills on a daily basis.
— Become free of alcohol/drug abuse.
— Learn to have difficult conversations with people without yelling, raising my voice, or interrupting while also learning to listen and better express my thoughts and emotions.

As you can see, these goals are rather broad, so it is helpful to create short-term goals that will help you achieve them. To do this, consider each of the steps you might need to take to reach these long-term goals. You then turn each of the steps you need to take into short-term goals. Such as:

— Learn to calm myself with deep breathing exercises.
— Learn to step back from stressful situations and calm myself with deep breathing.
— Learn to come back to a situation newly calmed and speak calmly.
— Learn to express my difficult feelings and thoughts without getting angry or raising my voice.

This is only a small sample of potential goals, as each person's goals will be different. The steps you need to take will vary based on what specific things you struggle with and other life circumstances. But, by creating a long-term goal and working backward to figure out what steps need to be taken, you can more easily create helpful short-term goals.

One of the first steps you should take in anger management is setting goals. That means once you finish this book, you can sit down with a piece of paper and start figuring out your individual goals. If you are unsure what anger goals to set, try asking those close to you what areas you could improve in with your anger. This will allow you to see what areas your anger burdens them, allowing you to take steps to improve and lessen the burden.

Diet

We've all heard the phrase "you are what you eat," and the truth is that what you eat does not only affect your physical well-being but your mental well-being, as well! This is especially true of people who consume stimulants, such as caffeine, which can be found in coffee, tea, chocolate, and soda. Anyone with anger issues should be careful with these foods, as stimulants increase the stress hormone, which thereby increases anger. Generally, it is better to keep a healthy and balanced diet. If you are eating a diet that causes your blood sugar to fluctuate drastically or you skip meals, then you will again experience increased stress and anger.

Skipping meals might appear to be a good idea to some when you are trying to lose weight, but it has detrimental effects on your hormones and stress. It is better to eat smaller meals more frequently than to go long periods without food. Avoid excessive alcohol intake, and avoid alcohol altogether if you have a drinking problem. While people often drink when they are feeling down—a bad habit—alcohol is actually a depressant, meaning it will make your mood even worse. Along with that, it can stimulate anger and cause dehydration, which will only worsen your mood further. In general, follow standard health guidelines when it comes to a healthy balanced diet. You can ask your doctor for any specific dietary guidelines that you might need to consider if you have any health conditions.

Self-Management Strategies

Oftentimes, when we are struggling with thoughts of anger, we are dealing with a repeat of the same or similar thoughts. In times such as this, it can be helpful to have go-to phrases you can use to remind yourself what to do. These thoughts can be used spur-of-the-moment. They are not a replacement for other tools and methods, such as deep breathing and cognitive restructuring. Rather, you can use these helpful reminders along with or until you are able to use other methods to help. For best results, you should have a week or two worth of completed anger log worksheets so that you can see what you frequently struggle with in black-and-white. You want to create nine categories of helpful thoughts so that you always have a helpful phrase on hand.

These categories include:

— Explanations – Rather than assuming the worst of people, these thoughts allow you to consider things from their side. Why might they be making the choice that they are?

— Accuracy – Reminders to not exaggerate or magnify a situation, to instead focus on the facts.

— The Whole Picture – This helps you to avoid overgeneralization or labeling, to help you see the whole picture rather than focusing on a single area.

— Problem-Solving – Reminder to look for solutions other than anger.

— Self-Confidence – Remember to not look down on yourself. You are trying your best, and you have the tools you need to succeed at anger management.

— Stay Cool – Remember to calm down and use your anger management techniques.

— Escape Routes – Remember to take a break or walk away from a situation rather than getting angry.

— Doing Their Best – Reminder that everyone has their own struggles and are trying their best.

— My Preference – Reminder that "should" statements are harmful. You might have a preference, but that doesn't mean other people "should" follow them.

On a piece of paper, write out each of the nine categories above. Underneath each of the categories, write two to five phrases that serve their given purpose based on your completed anger logs. These are a great tool because you create the phrases you know will help you the most based on your lived experience. For instance, for the category Say Cool, one person might find "just count to three and breathe" helpful while another person may find "This will be over soon and everything will be okay, there is no reason to get angry" more helpful. Once you are done writing out your various thoughts, put them somewhere, you can easily access them. Some people might simply keep a copy of the paper on them, while others might prefer to transfer the information to their phone. It doesn't matter how you keep it, as long as you have it on hand as a reminder when needed.

Relapse Prevention

In order to avoid relapse, you have to realize that you have to be proactive in avoiding relapse and create a plan. Ideally, you want to make a few short lists detailing areas you might face problems and what you can do about them. For instance, it might look like this:

— Anger management technique to do daily – Meditation, deep breathing, mindfulness.
— Ways to calm down when stressed – Deep breathing, mindfulness, etc.
— People who will hold me accountable – Mom, dad, spouse, anger support group.
— Motivations to stick to scheduled techniques and goals – If I miss a day of my techniques, I'm fined $10 that I give to [another person.] If I meet a short-term goal, I reward myself with my favorite ice cream. If I meet a long-term goal, I reward myself with a new video game.

Once you create your list, you should pin it somewhere that you can easily see it. For instance, you might place it on the wall of your office, on the front of your fridge, or on your bathroom wall. You want it to be somewhere that it is a constant reminder so that you are less likely to become lax. The fines and rewards will also help with that.

WORKBOOK PAGES

Print out these pages for easy use in managing your anger. Keep them on hand so that you can easily use them at a moments notice.

Anger Log

Date/Time:	
Trigger:	
Warning Signs:	
Response:	
Outcome:	

Cognitive Restructuring Worksheet

Situation:	
Thoughts:	
Emotions:	
Behaviors:	
Alternative Thought:	

Contingency Plan Worksheet

Potential Problem:	
Solution:	

Potential Problem:	
Solution:	

Potential Problem:	
Solution:	

Core Belief Worksheet

Thought to question:

Is there evidence to support it? Evidence against it?

Is it based on facts or feelings?

Am I making assumptions or misinterpreting evidence?

Am I seeing the nuances or am I viewing it in black-and-white?

Am I looking at all the evidence or only that which supports my belief?

Could I be exaggerating the truth?

Would other people interpret it differently? How?

Is the thought likely or a worst case scenario?

Am I having this thought out of habit or is it supported by facts?

New Balanced Thought:

Identifying and Correcting Distortion

1. In the spaces provided below, fil in details of anger provoking situations in your everyday life, along with the thoughts that exemplify each anger distortion listed;
2. Name the countermeasures (balanced thoughts) that you would employ for the anger distortions that you have listed

Overgeneralization		
Situations	Thoughts	Countermeasures

All-or-Nothing Thinking

Situations	Thoughts	Countermeasures

Discounting the Positive

Situations	Thoughts	Countermeasures

Magnification

Situations	Thoughts	Countermeasures

Mental Filters

Situations	Thoughts	Countermeasures

Jumping to Conclusions

Situations	Thoughts	Countermeasures

Emotional Reasoning

Situations	Thoughts	Countermeasures

Labeling

Situations	Thoughts	Countermeasures

Personalization and Blame

Situations	Thoughts	Countermeasures

"Should" Statements

Situations	Thoughts	Countermeasures

Imaginal Anger Exposure Worksheet

Situation:

Interpretation:

Anger Rating: (0-100)

| 10 | 20 | 30 | 40 | 50 | 60 | 70 | 80 | 90 | 100 |

Coping Mechanism:

The Relaxation Procedure

"Get into a comfortable position, close your eyes, and sit quietly for a few seconds, taking some slow, deep breaths.

Lower arms

Build up the tension in your lower arms by making fists with your hands and pulling up on your wrists. If your nails are long, press your fingers against your palms to make fists. Feel the tension through your lower arms, wrists, fingers, knuckles, and hands. Focus on the tension. Notice the sensations of pulling, of discomfort, of tightness. Hold the tension (10 seconds). Now, release the tension and let your hands and lower arms relax onto the chair or bed, with your palms facing down. Focus your attention on the sensations of relaxation in your hands and arms. Feel the release from tension. Relax the muscles (20 seconds), and as you relax, breathe smoothly and slowly from your abdomen. Each time you exhale, think the word "relax."

Upper arms

Now, build up the tension in your upper arms by pulling your arms back and in, toward your sides. Feel the tension in the back of your arms and radiating up into your shoulders and back. Focus on the sensations of tension. Hold the tension (10 seconds). Now, release your arms and let them relax. Focus on your upper arms, and feel the difference compared with the tension. Your arms might feel heavy, warm, and relaxed. As you relax (20 seconds), breathe smoothly and slowly from your abdomen. Each time you exhale, think the word relax.

Lower legs

Now, build up the tension in your lower legs by flexing your feet and pulling your toes toward your upper body. Feel the tension as it spreads through your feet, ankles, shins, and calves. Focus on the tension spreading down the back of your leg, into your foot, under your foot, and around your toes. Concentrate on that part of your body (10 seconds). Now, release the tension. Let your legs relax heavily onto the chair or bed. Feel the difference in the muscles as they relax. Feel the release from tension, the sense of comfort, and the warmth and heaviness of relaxation (20 seconds). As you breathe smoothly and slowly, think the word "relax" each time you exhale.

Upper legs

Build up the tension in your upper legs by pulling your knees together and lifting your legs off of the bed or chair. Focus on the tightness in your upper legs. Feel the pulling sensations from the hip down, and notice the tension in your legs. Focus on that part of your body (10 seconds). Now, release the tension, and let your legs drop down heavily onto the chair or bed. Let the tension go away. Concentrate on the feeling of relaxation. Feel the difference in your legs. Focus on the feeling of comfort (20 seconds), and as you breathe smoothly and slowly, think the word "relax" each time you exhale.

Abdomen

Now, build up the tension in your stomach by pulling your stomach in toward your spine very tightly. Feel the tension. Feel the tightness, and focus on that part of your body (10 seconds). Now, let your stomach relax outwards. Let it go further and further. Feel the sense of warmth circulating across your stomach. Feel the comfort of relaxation (20 seconds). As you breathe smoothly and slowly, think the word "relax" each time you exhale.

Chest

Now, build up the tension around your chest by taking a deep breath and holding it. Your chest is expanded, and the muscles are stretched around it. Feel the tension in your chest and back. Hold your breath (10 seconds). Now, slowly, let the air escape and breathe normally, letting the air flow in and out smoothly and easily. Feel the difference as the muscles relax compared with the tension, and think the word "relax" each time you exhale.

Shoulders

Imagine that your shoulders are on strings and are pulled up toward your ears. Feel the tension around your shoulders, radiating down into your back and up into your neck and the back of your head. Focus on this part of your body. Concentrate on the sensations around your neck and shoulders (10 seconds), and then let your shoulders droop. Relax and let them droop further and further. Feel the sense of relaxation around your neck and shoulders. Concentrate on the sensation of relaxation (20 seconds) in this part of your body. As you breathe smoothly and slowly, think the word "relax" each time you exhale.

Neck

Build up the tension around your neck by pressing the back of your neck toward the chair or bed and pulling your chin down toward your chest. Feel the tightness around the back of your neck spreading up into the back of your head. Focus on the tension (10 seconds). Now, release the tension, letting your head rest comfortably against the bed or chair. Concentrate on the relaxation (20 seconds), and feel the difference from the tension. As you breathe smoothly and slowly, think the word "relax" each time you exhale.

Mouth, Throat and Jaw

Build up the tension around your mouth, jaw, and throat by clenching your teeth and forcing the corners of your mouth back into a forced smile (10 seconds). Feel the tightness, and concentrate on the sensations. Then, release the tension, letting your mouth drop open and the muscles around your throat and jaw relax. Concentrate on the difference in the sensations in that part of your body (20 seconds). As you breathe smoothly and slowly, think the word "relax" each time you exhale.

Eyes

Build up the tension around your eyes by squeezing your eyes tightly shut for a few seconds, and then releasing. Then, let the tension around your eyes slide away. Feel the difference as the muscles relax (20 seconds). As you breathe smoothly and slowly, think the word "relax" each time you exhale.

Lower forehead

Build up the tension across your lower forehead by frowning, pulling your eyebrows down and toward the center. Feel the tension across your forehead and the top of your head. Concentrate on the tension (10 seconds), and then release, smoothing out the wrinkles and letting your forehead relax. Feel the difference as you relax (20 seconds). As you breathe smoothly and slowly, think the word "relax" each time you exhale.

Upper forehead

Build up the tension across your upper forehead by raising your eyebrows as high as you can. Feel the wrinkling and pulling sensations across your forehead and the top of your head. Hold the tension (10 seconds), and then relax, letting your eyebrows rest and the tension leave. Concentrate on the sensations of relaxation, and feel the difference in comparison to tension. As you breathe smoothly and slowly, think the word "relax" each time you exhale.

Now your whole body is feeling relaxed and comfortable. As you feel yourself becoming even more relaxed, count from one to five.

One, letting all of the tension leave your body. Two, sinking further and further into relaxation. Three, feeling more and more relaxed. Four, feeling very relaxed. Five, feeling deeply relaxed. As you spend a few minutes in this relaxed state, think about your breathing. Feel the cool air as you breathe in and the warm air as you breathe out. Your breathing is slow and regular. Every time you breathe out, think the word "relax" (2 minutes). Now, count backward from five, gradually feeling yourself become more alert and awake. Five, feeling more awake. Four, coming out of the relaxation. Three, feeling more alert. Two, opening your eyes. One, sitting up."

Relaxation record

Rate relaxation and concentration at the end of each practice, using the following scale:

10	20	30	40	50	60	70	80	90	100
None		Mild		Moderate		Strong		Excellent	

Date	Relaxation at the end of the Exercise	Concentration During the Exercise

Problem-Solving Worksheet

Problem:

Goal:

Proceeding Options:

Potential Consequences:

Decision:

Relapse Prevention Worksheet

Daily Management Tasks:

Weekly Management Tasks:

Calming Tools:

People Holding Me Accountable:

Motivation:

CONCLUSION

Anger is not something you can overcome instantly, especially if you have experienced unmanaged anger for a long period of time. It has become a habit that is deeply wired in you. But, that does not mean it is impossible, only that you can't expect instant results. If you put in the work, following the advice, and practicing the techniques in this book, you will see growth and improvement if you put in consistent effort and hard work. With daily effort, you will get closer to your goals. It is easy to be impatient, which can worsen anger.

So, to lessen your impatience for immediate results, flip ahead on the calendar three months from today and circle the date. Along with this, write out a list of your anger issues and shortcomings that you can see that you have at this point in time. Seal the list in an envelope and put it somewhere safe. During the next three months, continue putting in the hard work, following the advice of this book, but holding off on worrying about the results.

In three months' time, open the envelope and see how far you have come with your consistent effort. I am sure that you will see many areas from the list that you have improved on, and you might see even more growth that you never considered writing down. By working hard for three months, regardless of the results, you are sure to grow and improve your anger management. Thank you for reading this book! You now have the tools you need to manage your anger and experience a better life. I hope that you find success on your journey.

APPENDIX

The Origin and Evolution of CBT

Through the past century, there have been a vast number of groundbreaking scientific and medicinal discoveries that have changed the way of life for people worldwide. These discoveries do not just relate to technology and physical health but mental health as well. These discoveries include the roots of what is now known as cognitive-behavioral therapy or CBT. In this chapter, we will be exploring the origin, evolution, modern usage, and future of CBT—and its many amazing benefits! By learning more about these aspects of CBT, you can better learn how it can be implemented for mental growth, healing, and success.

While CBT is usually referred to as a singular form a therapy, the truth is that it is a collection of therapies and techniques used in conjunction with one another. These techniques have an empirically-backed proof of effectiveness, leading back to the 1940s when the methods were first used in conjunction with leading psychologists. This is an important time for CBT because while certain techniques used take root prior to this time, it was in the '40s when psychologists were treating vets who returned with what was then known as "shell shock" that they first started putting the puzzle pieces of various therapies together to create a new form of therapy. During this time, soldiers all over the world were struggling to adjust to their mental health after returning home from war. Not only was it a difficult adjustment after the trauma they had just endured, but the world at large didn't understand their struggle. Often times, soldiers with shell shock, what is now known as a post-traumatic stress disorder, would be seen as "weak" or "cowards," therefore reducing the likelihood of them getting the help they so desperately needed.

Thankfully, World War II vets and psychologists at the time worked together. The psychologists themselves were able to create treatment plans using their expertise, but the vets also did their part in seeking help, being open, taking steps to work through their trauma, and facing the social prejudices. It's essential to keep in mind that any healing a person receives due to therapy, no matter the type, is not only the success of the therapist. Yes, the therapist works hard with the patient, but no amount of therapy will help if the patient does not take the steps to betterment themselves. It is in this way that the early-day vets and psychologists were able to work through the social stigmas and ignorance to develop CBT, not only for PTSD but for the treatment of other mental health disorders, as well. Two of the early pioneers of cognitive-behavioral therapy are Dr. Ellis and Dr. Beck, both of which are famous in psychotherapy circles for their contributions to the field.

However, before these two doctors could build the foundation for what would become CBT, they were inspired by even earlier pioneers of their time. To understand how CBT would be developed later on, it is necessary that we look back at these early pioneers and their groundbreaking research. You have likely heard of Pavlov's Dog, which is a famous experiment that many people, even unfamiliar with psychology and therapy, are familiar with. What you might not be cognizant of is that this experiment and the principles it is based on—known as classical conditioning—is one of the many building blocks that would lead to the creation of CBT. But, for those who may be unaccostomed with Pavlov's Dog, the experiment was conducted in order to study the salivation of dogs when fed. Specifically, Pavlov was studying how much saliva in volume dogs would salivate when given food. As frequently happens with scientific breakthroughs, Pavlov found unexpected findings that would become a pivotal aspect of classical conditioning—also known as responsive conditioning. When beginning the experiment, Pavlov, a Russian researcher, theorized that the dogs would begin to salivate whenever they were fed. However, he quickly discovered that the dogs would begin to salivate before the food even arrived.

As soon as the dogs heard the approaching footsteps of the researchers, they would begin to salivate. This discovery promoted Pavlov to further investigate the dog's association with food and whether they would salivate; and, as many people are aware, the dogs would begin to salivate with anything that reminded them of being fed, whether it was the footsteps of the approaching researchers or a ringing bell. Pavlov realized the importance of this discovery and dedicated the remainder of his career to researcher and experiment with classical conditioning.

Classical conditioning does not only apply to dogs but humans, as well. In short, this discovery proved that people (and animals) could begin to associate specific stimulus or signals with a naturally occurring event. In Pavlov's Dog, the dogs begin to associate the sound of footsteps or bells with being fed, thus causing the natural response of drooling. This can be applied to many circumstances. For instance, when a parent is potty training their young child, they may give them a piece of candy whenever they successfully use the toilet. The child will begin to associate the desired activity with getting candy, promoting them to continue using the toilet as they have been conditioned to believe that they will be rewarded with something good when they succeed.

The first application of researchers utilizing classical conditioning with children is with another famous experiment, known as Little Albert. This experiment was conducted by the famed behaviorist Dr. John B. Watson and his then-graduate student, Rosalie Rayner. Using Pavlov's research, Watson sought to prove that classical conditioning could also elicit emotional responses in humans. Throughout the course of the study, Watson and Rayner would expose baby Albert to various stimuli, such as animals, masks, and fire; and then observe his reactions.

During the initial exposures, Albert did not appear to be afraid. However, during the following interactions, every time the child was exposed to a white rat, Watson would scare the child by loudly hitting a metal pipe and hammer to cause an alarming sound. This sound would scare the child, resulting in crying. Before long, baby Albert would cry whenever he saw the rat. This showed that baby Albert had made a connection between the rat and the noise, knowing that if he saw the rat, the noise was sure to follow, so he would begin to cry at the mere sight of the familiar fear.

While this experiment is famous, it is not due to positive reasons. Sure, the study proved classical conditions can affect human emotions. But, it raised many ethical concerns about the treatment of baby Albert. The child was harmed in the process of the experiment, inducing fear. The experiment was also not objectively sound, as Watson and Rayner relied on their own subjective interpretations of baby Albert rather than developing an objective means of observation. Simply put, this experiment would not be allowed in modern-day research.However, while the experiment of Little Albert may have been unethical, it was only the beginning of the research of classical conditioning in humans. The research it would lead to would help develop cognitive-behavioral therapy, as it would show that there is a connection between stimuli and response. Thus, psychotherapists would be able to treat their patients with anxiety disorders, substance abuse, or a number of other conditions by learning how to adjust the response to given stimuli until it becomes conditioned in a patient.

Along with classical conditioning, instrumental conditioning also played a role in the development of cognitive-behavioral therapy. This form of conditioning, also known as operant conditioning, is the use of positive or negative reinforcement to attain specific behavior goals. You can easily see examples of this in everyday life. For instance, if a child is praised and listened to when speaking to their parent, they are more likely to speak to them openly and honestly in the future. However, if a child is yelled at and chastised when they speak, they are more likely to learn to keep their distance and avoid any tough conversational topics.

The parents are either reinforcing or reducing the likelihood of their child speaking to them in the future, all depending on their behavior. This is just one instance of instrumental conditioning, but it plays out in countless ways in our daily lives. It was psychologist E.L. Thorndike that discovered instrumental conditioning through puzzle and reward experiments with cats. You have probably seen a variation of this experiment played out before, as it is commonly conducted with rats and other animals. In this case, the animal is placed in a maze or puzzle and must complete the task in order to receive food or get free. With Thorndike's experiment, when first placed in a puzzle box, the cats would panic and try to escape. But, over time, the cats learned that they could get out and be fed if they completed the puzzle. This lead to reduced anxiety, as the cats no longer felt trapped, and their response time to complete the puzzle rapidly increased. This process was named the Law of Effect, meaning that a response is likely to increase if it is followed by positive reinforcement and likely to decrease if it results in a negative response.

After Thorndike's instrumental conditioning experiments that would become a part of the behavioral therapy method, B.F. Skinner would continue the research. Skinner created a puzzle box much like the one used in Thorndike's experiments, which would become known as the Skinner Box. Working off of Thorndike's and Pavlov's research, Skinner was able to identify two main types of behavior. The first of the two is known as respondent behavior. With this type of behavior, a person will react reflexively to given stimuli without any prior conditioning. For instance, if you get something in your eye, you will rub your eyes, trying to get it out. If a bright light suddenly shines in your face, you will squint. If you touch something hot, you will drawback. If you begin to step on something, you will try to lighten your step and dodge it.

These are natural behaviors that humans instinctively have. The second of the two types of behavior is operant. This is a type of behavior that is learned. For instance, a person may not be scared of monkeys, but if a monkey injures the person badly or at a young age, then the person is likely to develop a learned response to fear the monkey. Similarly, through operant behavior, a person can also learn to react positively to specific stimuli if a positive association is created. Skinner was able to realize the potential of classical conditioning with operant and respondent behaviors for learning, an avenue of its application that Pavlov did not pursue.

Skinner was so passionate about the subject that he lead the development of learning through classical conditioning in the United States. In order to further his knowledge and its teaching, Skinner published a book on the subject in 1953, titled Science and Human Behavior. Psychologist C. L. Hull made great progress in the field of behaviorism, as he created the Theory of Learning, otherwise known as the Drive Reduction Theory. This theory states that humans act on their drives of need, such as feelings of hunger, thirst, heat or cold, sexual desire, and more. Once a person is able to gain what they need to satisfy these desires, the need to fulfill the drive is reduced, thus reinforcing the behavior that leads to satisfying the desire. This can be used to help a person learn through the process of deprivation and reinforcement. Along with Skinner, following the end of World War II, there was another psychologist doing similar work. In South Africa,

Joseph Wolpe was one of several famed scientists who worked to develop classical conditioning at the time for the treatment of "shell shock"/post-traumatic stress disorder. In order to treat his patients struggling with phobias and anxiety, he sought a treatment approach that would desensitize the patient to a given stressor rather than a psychoanalytical approach—using the research of C. L. Hull's Theory of Learning and Pavlov's classical conditioning. In order to help a person struggling with anxiety or phobia, Wolpe would introduce specific stimuli in a controlled and safe environment, essentially using classical conditioning as a means of exposure therapy. While now known as cognitive behavioral therapy, during the early days of development, it was simply known as behavioral therapy. During this time of development, psychologists worked specifically to find effective therapies that could be used for a short or moderate length of time to help the struggling vets healthfully navigate their trauma and mental health needs. The collection of therapies they put together were a breakthrough, as prior to this point, the knowledge and treatment of PTSD, or shell shock, was practically unheard of. As you can see, the early roots of CBT were planted not by one but by many expert psychologists and behaviorists. The work of behaviorists and psychologists gave the entire psychotherapeutic community a more in-depth understanding of human conditioning and behaviors. It is the work of these early-day pioneers that would allow for psychologists later on to develop our modern-day cognitive-behavioral therapy.

Hans Eysenck continued to develop the budding psychotherapeutic methods of the time with his own team of psychologists at the Maudsley Institute—one of the leading institutes in London. One of

Eysenck's strongly held beliefs was that the therapeutic psychoanalysis method as popularized at the time by Sigmund Freud was non-scientific and simply nothing more than a placebo. Eysenck theorized in his published book that the only effective and scientifically-sound form of psychotherapy is one based on modern learning theory methods, such as behavioral and cognitive therapies. His work at the institute solidified the use of behavioral and cognitive-behavioral therapies in the United Kingdom. Along with his development of the Maudsley Institute, another great impact that Eysenck had was in the foundation of the scientific journal, Behaviour Research, and therapy.

This journal allowed for countless people in the field to have an outlet to develop and share their work and breakthroughs in behavior therapy. This development, in turn, allowed for more psychotherapists worldwide to learn about behavior therapy and implement it in their own practice. Once the initial version of CBT, then known as behavioral therapy, was created in the 1940s, it continued to be built upon and improved over the next couple of decades. Because of this, there is not one singular point in time where you can definitely say that CBT originated without examining it further.

After all, much of the behavioral evidence took root a couple of decades prior to its use in the '40s and then was further built upon in the following decades. In the 1950s and '60s, behavioral therapy saw great improvement thanks to the work of Albert Ellis, to the point that he is now known as a pioneer in the field. Many aspects of CBT that are used today, such as identifying irrational thoughts, challenging said thoughts, and promoting a more rational thought process, were all used by Dr. Ellis in use therapeutic treatment of patients. During his development of the techniques, Dr. Ellis even created a technique that is still used today, known as the ABC technique—which is one of the most widely used methods for identifying irrational and harmful thoughts. Another pioneer in CBT is Dr. Aaron T. Beck, who helped with the development into the 60s so much that he is now known as a founding father of cognitive-behavioral therapy. The importance of his research really can not be overstated. He changed the course for psychotherapy worldwide, leading to him being named one of the top five most influential psychotherapists.

During his research in the 60s, Dr. Beck was working on experiments to test his psychological beliefs at the University of Pennsylvania, which would become groundbreaking. The results of these experiments allowed him to find methods of CBT that most help patients struggling with long-term depression. Dr. Beck found that many patients with depression would struggle with regular and reoccurring negative thoughts. These thoughts frequently didn't appear to be triggered by outward circumstances or worry but instead appeared spontaneously. For instance, a person might frequently have the thought, "I am worthless," without any specific outward circumstances causing them to feel this way. They don't feel that they are worthless because they failed to reach a goal, though that could certainly exacerbate the feelings; rather, they struggle with these negative thoughts regardless of their outward circumstances. The person might have succeeded in meeting their goal and still feel worthless.

As Dr. Beck worked with numerous patients, he was able to find commonalities in their thought patterns. He discovered that when a patient struggled with depression, they usually experienced negative thoughts in three different categories. These negative thoughts included feelings of inadequacies of oneself, fear of failure, and fear of the future. By coming to understand this aspect of depression, Dr. Beck began to find new ways to view and treat depression than what was standard at the time. With this understanding, he helped his patients to directly confront these negative thoughts that were obstructing their healing. He was able to help teach his patients how to reframe their negative thoughts into something more balanced and positive, allowing them to slowly overcome their thoughts and feelings.

The benefits of the therapy Dr. Beck provided did not cease when a patient's therapy sessions ended, either. Instead, it was found that by teaching a patient to reframe their thoughts, they could experience genuine change and long-lasting improvements.

Dr. Aaron Beck's work did not end with him. Together with his daughter, he founded The Beck Institute for Cognitive Behavior Therapy, in which doctors were able to make further groundbreaking discoveries in psychotherapy treatment, which would become a standard global resource when learning about CBT. While working at the institute, Dr. Aaron Beck's daughter, Dr. Judith Beck, was able to pioneer in CBT herself, focusing on the use of positive coping mechanisms for growth.

Dr. Albert Bandura, a Canadian-American psychologist, further developed cognitive-behavioral therapy in the 1970s. Bandura focused on the model of social learning theory in his work. In summary, this theory states that the cognitive process is of equal importance to a person's behavior. He believed that while the direct experience was the main factor in learning, it was not the sole factor, as learning could also be achieved through the judgment process. Bandura established the theory known as Reciprocal Determinism. This theory states that a person's cognition, behavior, and personal environmental factors are all of equal importance. These three factors can continuously reinforce others. To produce the desired change in these factors, Bandura believed that self-efficacy is the primary determining cognitive construct required and should thus be used in therapeutic interventions.

This lead to Bandura's theory being largely incorporated into behavioral therapy. Although while it does also affect behavioral-cognitive therapy, it has not been incorporated to the same extent. The reason for this is because Bandura believed that self-efficacy was best produced through behavioral accomplishment rather than verbal persuasion, and this belief is more suited to behavioral therapeutic methods than cognitive ones. The first period of the rapid development of behavioral therapy in the 1940s is frequently known as the "first wave" of its development, with further waves following. The second wave occurred in the 1960s, where the methods used continued to grow, gain notoriety, and undergo empirical testing. Due to the rapid speed at which psychotherapists began to gain a greater understanding of cognition, this phase in time is also sometimes known as the "cognitive revolution."

One way that cognitive-behavioral therapy developed during this time was by the advent of attribution theory. This theory purposefully examined the various complex thought processes in how people think both about themselves and others. It analyzes how a person may attribute something in their lives either to their own actions or the actions of others, even if neither party is necessarily responsible. For instance, a child may attribute their parents' divorce to their own actions, believing that they are to blame when, in reality, the child is not the cause of the divorce.

While this might be a more extreme and obvious example, especially to an adult without similar burdens, we all can experience such attributions at various scales throughout our lives. We may blame ourselves for failing to meet a deadline—even if the failure was due to outside circumstances out of our control. Or, we may blame a family member for something bad happening in our lives, regardless of where the responsibility lies. As you can imagine, there are countless ways in which a person experiences attribution of blame in daily life. By coming to understand the theory of attribution and how a person's conscious thoughts affect behavior, it gave psychotherapists a way to better understand and treat their patients.

It was during this period of the second wave of behavioral therapy that the name changed to what is now known as cognitive behavioral therapy—all due to the new understanding of human cognition. By combining the behavioral knowledge gained in the 40s and the cognition discoveries learned in the 60s, countless psychotherapists over the decades were able to create an amazing series of empirically-backed techniques that became CBT. These techniques are not only still used to this day, but they have actually become even more well-known as they continue to be proven as an effective treatment method for a variety of mental illnesses and struggles.

The Contemporary CBT Approach

At the time of writing this book, we are now in the third wave of cognitive-behavioral therapy understanding. This wave is not as rapid as the previous two, which occurred practically back-to-back in the 40s and 60s, as this wave has been ongoing for approximately the past fifteen or twenty years. But, just because the third wave of CBT understanding is more gradual doesn't mean it is any less profound and impactful. This is because the third wave has resulted in a boom of not only an increased understanding of human cognition and behavior but many types of methods and therapies that fit under the CBT umbrella, as well.

There are many forms of therapy that fit under this so-called umbrella that has been implemented in the third wave of CBT therapy. Just a handful of the more popular methods include Dialectical Behavior Therapy (DBT), Acceptance and Commitment Therapy (ACT), Mindfulness-Based Cognitive Therapy (MBCT), and many more! While each of these types of therapies has its own names and abbreviations, they still fall under the CBT umbrella and can be used in conjunction with each other or independently. In the contemporary or third-wave approach of CBT, psychotherapists put less emphasis on controlling or changing outward circumstances and experiences and instead focus on a person's internal cognitive response. For instance, many of the methods used will focus on mindfulness, acceptance, thought replacement, and flexibility. There are many ways this may play out in an individual patient's life, depending on the exact method of CBT a therapist employs along with what their specific struggles and goals for improvement are.

The Future Direction of CBT

When it comes to psychotherapy methods, cognitive behavioral therapy is widely known as the hallmark method, and its renown will likely only increase in the future. The reason for this is because CBT is highly adaptive to the individual. CBT is used in the treatment of a wide array of psychologically-based conditions. It is used to achieve long-lasting results in a short period. Lastly, it has regularly been proven through empirical research to be one of the most effective therapy methods in the field.

In one meta-analysis from 2013, researchers were able to identify studies analyzing the effects of CBT on many disorders. Some examples include insomnia, depression, anxiety disorders, substance abuse, schizophrenia, eating disorders, anger and aggression, bipolar disorder, psychotic disorders, general behavior, and even criminal behavior—and this is only the tip of the iceberg! The meta-analysis found many other disorders and problems that CBT has been used to treat and manage. CBT is frequently used to help a wide range of people, whether they are mentally ill and struggling with a disorder or even if they don't have a mental disorder and are instead struggling with another problem, such as anger or criminal behaviors. This meta-analysis found that cognitive-behavioral therapy is amazingly effective in treating all of these disorders and problems, and more! But, the strongest evidence for CBT and its benefits came in studies for general stress, anger, anxiety disorders, eating disorders, and somatic symptom disorders—in which the participants experienced exceptional results. In some studies, it has been found that CBT is as effective as anti-depressants for many people. This is great news for people whose medication alone is not enough, and for those who may be unable to take medication for whatever reason. But, this does not only mean that CBT can be used instead of anti-depressants and anti-anxiety medicines in certain cases; it also means that the two can be used together for even better results than either option alone.

Remember, whether a person uses medication or not is up to them and their doctor. While a person may not wish to take medication, they may need it due to a physical disturbance, such as a hormonal imbalance. In the same way, a person may wish to take medication but be unable to due to side effects. Whether you take medication or not, you should discuss it with your doctor, and never stop taking your medicine without first discussing it with them, as well. There is already a great amount of empirical evidence supporting CBT. But, in the future, we can expect further studies to continue to not only prove its effectiveness but better determine which problems and disorders CBT are most equipped to treat and how.

The public at large has been catching onto the effectiveness of CBT in recent years. While previously, people outside of the mental health field who have not gone to therapy likely would not have heard of CBT, more everyday people are becoming familiar with it. This is great news, as it enables more people to learn about the importance of their mental health and cognition. The increased awareness means that more people are likely to seek out CBT, empowering themselves to take control of their mental health, find the healing they desire and reach their goals. We can only hope that in the future, people will continue to learn about this importance and take the steps necessary for change with cognitive behavioral therapy.

BIBLIOGRAPHY

Anderson, R., Saulsman, L., & Nathan, P. (2011). Helping Health Anxiety. Perth, Western Australia: Centre for Clinical Interventions.

Barlow, D. H., Craske, M. G. (2000). Mastery of your anxiety and panic (3rd Edition). San Antonio, TX: The Psychological Corporation.

Barlow, D.H. (2002). Anxiety and Its Disorders: The Nature and Treatment of Anxiety and Panic (2nd Edition). Guilford Press

Bhave S. Y. and Saini S. (2009). Anger Management. Sage Publications

Burns, D.D. (1980). Feeling Good: The New Mood Therapy. New York: Signet

Clark D., Fairburn C., Hollon S.(2004). Oxford Guide to Behavioural Experiments in Cognitive Therapy. Oxford University Press.

Clark, D.A., Beck A.T. (2010). Cognitive Therapy of Anxiety Disorders. The Guilford Press

Clark, D.M. (1986). A cognitive approach to panic. Behav. Res. Ther. 24, No. 4. pp. 461-470.

Craske M.G. (2017). Cognitive Behavioral Therapy. Second edition. American Psychological Association. Washington, DC

Craske M.G., Barlow D.H. (2006). Mastery Of Your Anxiety And Worry. Second Edition. Workbook. Oxford University Press.

Craske, M. G., Barlow D. H. (2008). Panic Disorder and Agoraphobia. In Clinical Handbook of Psychological Disorders, Fourth Edition: A Step-by-Step Treatment Manual. Oxford University Press

Craske, M.G., Barlow, D.H. (2001). Panic disorder and agoraphobia. In D.H. Barlow (Ed.), Clinical Handbook Of Psychological Disorders, Third Edition. Guilford Press.

Dawson T. (2015). Anger Management. How to Deal With Your Anger, Frustration, and Temper to Avoid Anger Management Classes. CreateSpace Independent Publishing Platform

Dobson D., Dobson K.S. (2017). Evidence-Based Practice of Cognitive Behavioral Therapy. The Guilford Press

Dobson K.S., Dozois, D.J.A. (2019). Handbook of Cognitive Behavioral Therapies. The Guilford Press

Farmer, R.E., Chapman A.L. (2008). Behavioral Interventions in Cognitive Behavior Therapy. Practical guidance for putting theory into action. American Psychological Association

Faupel A., Herrick E., and Sharp P. (2011). Anger Management: A Practical Guide. Routledge

Fentz H.N et Al.. (2013). Mechanisms of change in cognitive behaviour therapy for panic disorder: The role of panic self-efficacy and catastrophic misinterpretations. Behaviour Research and Therapy 5, 579 e 587.

Freedman S., Adessky R. (2009). Cognitive Behavior Therapy for Panic Disorder. Isr J Psychiatry Relat Sci, 46 No.4 251–256.

Gentry, W. D. (2007). Anger Management for Dummies. Wiley Publishing, Inc.

Goldstein A.P., et al. (2004). New Perspectives on Aggression Replacement Training. John Wiley & Sons

Greene I. (2003). Anger Management for Men. P. S. I. Publishers

Greene I. (2003). Anger Management for Women. P. S. I. Publishers

Harvey, A.G. et al (2004). Cognitive Behavioural Processes Across Psychological Disorders: A Transdiagnostic Approach to Research and Treatment. Oxford University Press

Jones A., (1998) 104 Activities that Build: Self-Esteem, Teamwork, Communication, Anger Management, Self-Discovery, and Coping Skills. Rec Room Publishing

Ledley DR., Marx B.P., Heimberg, R.G.(2010). Making Cognitive-Behavioral Therapy Work Clinical Process for New Practitioners. Second Edition. The Guilford Press

Marris B. and Rae T. (2006). Teaching Anger Management and Problem-Solving Skills; Paul Chapman Publishing

McKay M., Rogers P. D.(2000). The Anger Control Workbook. New

Harbinger Publications

Nathan, P.R., Rees, C.S., Lim, L., & Smith, L.M. (2001). Mood Management – Anxiety: A Cognitive Behavioural Treatment Programme for Individual Therapy. Rioby Publishing.

Neudeck P., Wittchen .H (2012). Exposure Therapy: Rethinking the Model – Refining the Method. Springer

O'Donohue W., Fisher J.E. (2009). General Principles and Empirically Supported Techniques of Cognitive Behavior Therapy. Wiley & Sons

Otto M. W., and Smits J.A.J. (2011). Exercise for Mood and Anxiety. Proven Strategies for Overcoming Depression and Enhancing Well-Being. Oxford University Press

Otto M.W., Simon N.M., Olatunji B.O., Sung S.C., Pollack M.H. (2011). 10-Minute CBT: Integrating Cognitive-Behavioral Strategies into Your Practice. Oxford University Press

Puff R., Seghers J. (2014). The Everything Guide to Anger Management. Published by Adams Media

Prochaska, J. O, Norcross J.C., Ph.D. DiClemente C. C. (1994). Changing for Good. HarperCollins e-book

Reilly P. M., Shopshire, M. S. (2002). Anger Management for Substance Abuse and Mental Health Clients. U.S. Department of Health and Human Services

Saulsman, L., Nathan, P., Lim, L., Correia, H., Anderson, R., & Campbell, B. (2015). What? Me Worry!?! Mastering Your Worries. Perth, Western Australia: Centre for Clinical

Interventions.

Seiler, L. (2008). Cool Connections with Cognitive Behavioral Therapy. Jessica Kingsley Publishers London and Philadelphia

Teachman B.A., Marker C.D., and Clerkin E. M. (2010). Catastrophic misinterpretations as a predictor of symptom change during treatment for panic disorder. J. Consult, Clin. Psychol. December; 78(6): 964–973.

Wenzel A., Dobson K.,S., Hays P.,A (2016). Cognitive Behavioral Therapy Techniques and Strategies. American Psychological Association. Washington, DC

White, K.S. Barlow, D.H. (2002). Panic Disorder and Agoraphobia. In D.H. Barlow (Ed.), Anxiety and Its Disorders. Second Edition. Guilford Press

ABOUT THE AUTHOR

Antonio Matteo Bruscella is a psychologist and psychotherapist specialized in Cognitive Behavioral Therapy (CBT). Dr. Bruscella teaches at several schools of specialization in psychotherapy in Italy and is the Director of Education at the School of Specialization in Psychotherapy of Basilicata. He is president and a founding member of the Lucana Association of Psychology and Cognitive Behavioral Therapy (ALPTCC), ordinary member of the Italian Association of Behavior Analysis and Modification (AIAMC), and member of the British Psychological Society (BPS). His clinical and research interests are oriented towards the study and application of therapeutic protocols of evidence-based psychology. Dr. Bruscella has many years of clinical experience in the treatment of anxiety disorders and related emotional problems and is the author of numerous self-help publications in this field.

CBT SERIES

Made in the USA
Monee, IL
07 July 2021